Navigating the Fourth Dimension

A Discourse from the Ascended Masters St. Germain & El Morya Khan

Linda Stein-Luthke &
Martin F. Luthke, Ph.D.

Expansion Publishing

Navigating the Fourth Dimension

A Discourse from the Ascended Masters St. Germain & El Morya Khan

Linda Stein-Luthke &
Martin F. Luthke, Ph.D.

Photos by Martin S. Trimmer

ISBN 0-9656927-5-2

Expansion Publishing
P.O. Box 516 - Chagrin Falls, OH 44022
USA

Contents

: ♦ ♦ :

Foreword

There are some mysteries that I'm not telling you.
There's so much doubt everywhere, so many opinions
that say, "What you announce may be true
in the future, but not now."
But this form of universal truth that I see says,

This is not a prediction.

This is here, in this instant, cash in hand! [1]

Dear Reader,

The fact that you are interested in this book means that you are curious about the fourth dimension. We must admit that, less than six months before we began working on this new book, we had no idea what the fourth dimension was, or what it would mean to us personally. Years ago, we had read books that mentioned this concept, and some of our friends talked about it quite enthusiastically. However, we did not pay much attention at all to this concept. We were primarily focused on the information and coaching we were receiving from the Ascended Masters in our daily channeling sessions, and the Masters weren't talking about it -- or so it seemed.

---

[1] From *"Green Ears,"* **The Essential Rumi,** p.239 (translated by Coleman Banks, with John Moyne), Edison, NJ: Castle Books, 1997.

: ♦ ♦ :

However, at the beginning of last summer, we began receiving more explicit information about the fourth dimension. It was then that we finally realized that the Masters had been guiding us all along toward an understanding of this new reality.

During the summer, we took an extended car trip out west. For about three weeks we were relatively isolated from family, friends and the daily responsibilities of life. Without the normal concerns of earning our keep and caring for our home, pets, family, friends and clients, we were able to move into a place of harmony and balance. We experienced a steady connection with an uninterrupted flow of Light, which was providing us with a sustained experience of the essence of the fourth dimension. Indeed, we were riding on a stream that carried us easily through life with little stress, worry or disharmony.

At the time, it all seemed very easy to embrace. Upon return home, however, we had to contend once again with the challenges of life as we had known it. Soon we would lose the rhythm and easy connection to our Light. This felt even more uncomfortable after the relative ease that we had been enjoying so recently. The only answer, then, was to open to the guidance that could show us how to get back to the fourth dimension, so that this frequency of loving Light would carry us once again.

And so we wrote this book for our own sakes -- although we gladly share it with you. We have tested its precepts repeatedly and have found that they have carried us to a new place and a new way of being. We can say that it is possible to live in this world now and enjoy the beauty of the loving Light of the fourth dimension.

: ◆ ◆ :

You might think this is a selfish way to be, considering how difficult life is for so many. Yet, we are not indifferent or oblivious in the face of suffering. In fact, in our work as healers and counselors, we witness profound suffering every day. We have realized, however, that by attaching ourselves to the suffering, we help no one. Only by healing the suffering that we find within ourselves in response to the suffering we observe around us can we maintain a healing frequency. This then creates an opening for higher-vibrational energy to pour into this plane and transform our universe. That is what we have chosen to do.

We wish our readers to understand that we do not claim at this time to have fully mastered the lessons that are contained in this publication. Our own growth into a fourth-dimensional way of being has been uneven -- and unique for each of us. When we allow our ego-minds to regain dominance, states of pain and confusion temporarily return, providing further lessons in humility and compassion. Only when we realign ourselves with our Light are we able to regain the peace and harmony that we have come to treasure. Surrendering to one's Light is worth the "effort"!

As you open yourself to the blessings of the fourth dimension, we encourage you, above all, to be compassionate with yourself. Let the Light love you unconditionally. It is there already. It just asks for your willing acceptance of its healing and transforming energy.

Thank you for allowing us to share with you.

Love and Light, Linda & Martin

: ♦ ♦ :

About the Authors

We have found that it is often easier to relate to new information if you have at least a vague idea of the person or source it is coming from. So, before we get to the main topic of this book, let us take a minute to introduce ourselves.

The **Ascended Masters** are a group of Beings of Light who have gained complete awareness of their Totality. They once walked this Earth in human bodies and are now serving humanity and all of creation from the higher planes of existence, offering their Light, love and wisdom freely to all, at this auspicious time of accelerating change. The Ascended Masters **St. Germain** and **El Morya Khan** are the sources of inspiration behind this publication and its true authors.

Linda Stein-Luthke is the one who brought the following text to paper. Among the gifts she has chosen is the ability to "channel" wisdom from sources other than her human consciousness. Channeling is a process during which we open ourselves to higher vibrational frequencies of Light. The frequencies we access can be from our own being or from other beings of Light working in conjunction with us. For many years, Linda has been channeling highly evolved spiritual beings of Light, most frequently the Ascended Masters El Morya Khan and St. Germain, as well as the Light of the Christos and the Ma (a.k.a. Divine Mother) energy.

Linda has been a practitioner and teacher of astrology for more than twenty-five years. In addition, she works as a metaphysical teacher, healer and medical intuitive, using the various skills she

: ♦ ♦ :

has learned during her many years "on the path" and learning new ones every step of the way. She has been a mother and foster mother, successful business woman, activist and philanthropist in the women's community, and, first and foremost, a seeker throughout her life. She has traveled widely and has collaborated with masters from various parts of the world. Her training has been within the Hindu, Buddhist, Sufi, Christian, and Jewish faiths. Linda has been a presenter at national and international conferences, as well as a leader of workshops and trainings.

Linda channeled three earlier books by St. Germain, with the titles *Balancing the Light Within, Affirmations and Thought Forms* and *Angels and Other Beings of Light* (see appendix).

Dr. Martin Luthke is a clinical psychologist with in-depth training in traditional psychology and psychotherapy. His current practice, however, has shifted entirely to an energy-based paradigm. Together with his wife Linda, he has developed an advanced energy-psychological approach called Psychoenergetic Healing. Martin is the founder and director of the *Institute of Psychoenergetic Healing* and the (co-) author of several books and publications, among them *Riding the Tide of Change* and *Beyond Psychotherapy* (see appendix). He is a healer and metaphysical teacher, and has given workshops, trainings and presentations in the United States and Europe.

In addition, Martin is a publisher, skilled cabinetmaker, caretaker of home, garden and greenhouse, "Daddy" to three cats and a dog, and the husband of Linda for the past ten years.

: ♦ ♦ :

Martin took responsibility for the editing and production aspects of this collaborative project.[2]

More information about the authors and their work can be found on the web site *www.u-r-light.com.*

---

[2] We thank Julianne Stein for her invaluable contributions in the editing process and we thank Martin Trimmer for providing the cover photos.

: ♦ ♦ :

Navigating the Fourth Dimension

The Past No Longer Applies

You are living in a time of great change for your planet Earth and all who reside upon her. In fact, you have entered a new world, a new reality that we shall call the fourth dimension, for want of a better term. Of course, this cannot completely describe the new world that has opened up for you, but it is a useful term that allows you a greater awareness of what is presently occurring for you.

To introduce the term "fourth dimension," let us say that what you are reading on this page appears in two dimensions, the objects in the world around you appear to your physical senses in three dimensions, and what you can now perceive and know that is *not* so easily apparent to your physical senses is fourth-dimensional in nature. In time, however, you will be able to more easily perceive this dimension. This would include all that you might previously have called phenomenal, extrasensory, or even magical. What is happening for all humans -- and none is exempt from this experience -- is that the world you have always known is dissolving rapidly now. Very rapidly indeed. Concepts and precepts that you have all held dear and true, and which have appeared to be tried and true for millennia, are no longer so.

: ♦ ♦ :

To illustrate this point, may we take an excellent example of a time-tested third-dimensional concept, the concept of "war." For millennia now, human beings have waged war within a framework of certain assumptions that have been dear to them. Part of the rule book of waging war has been the concept of occupying the land of the vanquished with a great and terrible force, and thereby subduing, conquering and oppressing the original occupants of that land as you claim it for your own. During your last global war this concept still held true; the victorious powers laid to rest those who had attempted conquest and made the world "safe" once more with the tools of mass destruction and brute force.

Since that great global war, however, nothing has been quite the same. Indeed, what has happened as humanity has opened to its Light is that you can no longer win a war as you once did. You can no longer go in with brute force and conquer another land and its people. Instead, now you must take into consideration the brilliance of the Light that flows through each inhabitant of the land you are trying to conquer. You have to be aware that if the consensus of the inhabitants and the Light they carry is not in agreement with your act of brute force, you will not win that war. All the force you can manufacture in your third-dimensional world will never prevail over the fourth-dimensional energies of Light that are now flowing through all of humanity. This is not an edict that we state, this is simply what is so.

War is a third-dimensional concept. It has outlived its usefulness as a tool of the willful ego-mind of humans. If we may be so bold as to extrapolate, *every* institution that currently guides your existence is based on third-dimensional concepts that you, who are now evolving rapidly into a new species, will no longer find useful and will wish to eliminate in favor of new ways of being. What will replace the outmoded concepts and institutions will be very simple, in contrast to the world in which you have lived.

We offer you a new perspective, which you might find useful in dealing with your new world as we welcome you to it. This new world is accessible to you now; it is characterized by peace, harmony, balance, joy, unconditional love, and most important, an abundance of Light.

Now, you may ask, "If I am observing a world filled with pain, suffering, war, lack and all sorts of unhappy circumstances, how can you tell me that I can instead live, here and now, in the world of the fourth dimension that is peaceful, harmonious, balanced, joyful, loving and in an abundance of Light?" This does not make sense to the human mind, does it? Yet we will tell you that this is so.

This new publication is designed to teach you the tools that you, each and every one of you, can use to find this new world. And as always, the journey begins within.

Fear is the Obstacle

Beloved children, in the core of your being you are aware that great change is afoot upon your human plane. Some of what you have noticed so far may be encouraging, but most of what you have become aware of does not please you at all. If truth be known, for all of you, to consider such information appears to

: ◆ ◆ :

be most frightening. You do not like how things are -- but you aren't sure that the change we speak of will bring any improvement. What precedent do you have to believe that these changes could actually make things better?

Indeed, in Leia's case, it appears that her biggest concern will be whether there will still be running water and electricity. For her, if change implies that she must live in primitive conditions that may imperil the health of herself and her family, then she is not sure that this would be a good idea. Leia does not come from hardy stock, and she finds the comforts of the life she now enjoys very appealing. What she had learned about the changes on your planet implied that all the comforts of her current world would be taken away. This had been a frightening thought indeed.

And so, what we speak of now is *fear*. It is most useful for you to understand that the greatest enemy of your human form is this very concept: fear. We cannot emphasize this enough. For everything that you call "evil" on your human plane comes from a fear-based thought. *Everything*. Nothing that you have ever experienced as human beings that causes pain or suffering is exempt from this statement. And of course, what you call evil always involves pain and suffering. We need not dwell on what these things can be. You all know them well.

We must interject here that we do not label anything. From our vantage point we see all as Light. All and everything *is* Light. But on your Earth, dear children, you have labeled everything. It is you who call things "evil" and choose to live in fear. The fear then produces pain and suffering in your beings.

: ◆ ◆ :

You have chosen to live on a plane of freewill choice. What this means is that Infinite Source, the Light of all and everything, has allowed you to co-create all that you have chosen to experience. You have been given an opportunity to experience anything one could think of -- and you have let your thoughts run wild! Now you are entering a time when you may wish to consciously choose thoughts that free you of pain and suffering -- and that means thoughts that free you from fear.

Once it became apparent to Leia, through her own personal experience, that connection to the fourth dimension was an experience free of all fear, she then realized that all her fears concerning change could dissolve. Now she freely and joyously embraces the thought of change. She has even realized that, in this new dimension, if she needs water to run or light to illuminate her space, her needs will be met.

At this point, we have given you the basic answer to all that you need to know about this new dimension. But you will probably tell us that we have left out a few things. So, we apologize for this oversight and will step back a bit, and offer you more information that will lead you from fear-based thoughts -- which block your Light and access to the fourth dimension -- to thoughts that can free you to enjoy your new world.

Again, you may say to us, "Masters, how can this be true -- that I can free myself of these fears and thus be able, now, in this moment, to live in the fourth dimension, when all I see around me is suffering and pain? Indeed, I myself am still experiencing suffering and pain, so how can I be free of such and live in this dimension?" That is an excellent question, and the very question that keeps you from this experience.

: ◆ ◆ :

How can you live in the fourth dimension? If we were to tell you that it is easily done, you would not believe us. *The truth is simple* -- it is the human mind that is inclined to make it difficult. But we ask you to keep in mind that the truth is simple. Very simple indeed. It involves a group of concepts that you will have to embrace without reservation. In fact, you will have to *surrender* to these concepts with complete *trust*. Complete trust. And once you can do that, you will be free to enter this new frequency of Light. It can happen at any time. You will know when you are ready.

You Are in the Center of Your Universe

Beloved children, you live in the center of your universe. Did you know that? Perhaps not. What does this mean? Picture, if you will, a vast, spacious room, circular in nature. This room is empty. It is your universe, and as you place yourself in the center of it, you begin to fill it, simply by being there. As you place yourself in the center of this empty room, you bring with you all that you have ever been or ever will be. Some call this concept your "Higher Self." We will call it your "Totality." Encoded within this Totality is every thought and desire that you have ever had or ever will have. It is all and everything that is You. As you fill this empty room with You, and as you stand in its center, it becomes the universe in which you reside.

Just as no two humans are identical, so it is true of the universe in which you reside. You may think of your universe as a turtle shell that you carry on your back. Indeed, in some cultures this is exactly the image of the universe that is commonly accepted.

: ♦ ♦ :

What you choose to carry in your universe, as you move through lifetime after lifetime as human being, very much becomes your experience of the human plane. And just as no two human beings or universes are identical, this also is true of your experiences.

Let us take, for example, the book that you are reading. We will be so bold as to say that the preceding paragraphs will never mean exactly the same thing to any of you. Why might this be so? Because none of you has a history identical to that of anyone else, nor do you experience your history in identical ways, how you interpret the preceding words will be unique to you.

You may say, "Master, how can you tell us that we are all sharing movement into the fourth dimension as human beings on Earth, if we live in our own universes?" We can say this because the planet on whose back you ride is also having a unique experience as a living entity. This planet has chosen such movement, and you have chosen to be on the planet as this is happening; so we may say that you have all agreed to participate in this event. How you choose to *experience* this event, however, will be unique to you as you draw this event into your universe. Your Totality -- everything you have ever been or ever will be -- will determine how you respond to this event. Your response will be unique to you in your universe.

Let us take another example. Do you believe that the universe in which you live now is identical to the one in which your grandparents resided? What was the universe like, in their day? Did they know of such things as computers, or how to welcome advanced technology into their lives and use it to create change in their lifestyle? Wouldn't you agree that the universe they

: ◆ ◆ :

lived in was different from the one in which you reside today? Let us use another example: the different choices you all have made regarding places to live. Leia and Manalus just traveled through vast stretches of the United States, and they can attest that they saw terrain completely different from the land upon which they reside. They saw lifestyles totally unlike anything they have ever chosen to experience in this lifetime, and prior to encountering these things, all that they experienced on their trip was not part of their universe. Yet the people residing in those places live in those universes every day and do not know of the lifestyle of Leia and Manalus in their respective universes. This is truth.

Why do we ask you to understand this concept? Because before you can accept change -- and the healing of your fears that must accompany such change -- you must first understand that *change is possible*. You can accept the basic concept, if you choose, that the universe in which you reside has been created by *you,* by the choices you have made in lifetime after lifetime of existence on this planet. Prior to each embodiment, you reviewed your lifetimes and then chose what would bring you the greatest soul growth upon re-embodiment. That then has become the life you are leading now. Furthermore, you can accept, if you choose, that at this time it is easier than ever before for you to make new choices and allow yourself to reside in a new universe. That is so because you have chosen to be alive as the Earth is entering the fourth dimension where such things are possible. And further yet, you can choose -- when you are ready -- to allow this new universe to incorporate the characteristics of the fourth dimension that is now available to you. Are you willing to allow this to be so?

: ♦ ♦ :

Discussing the Mindset for Change

Beloved children, we have told you many things already, have we not? Some of what you have learned so far does appear useful to you, some of it does not. This idea of a new dimension being available to you, where you can go to live in peace, harmony and balance, does sound inviting, but it appears to be incongruous to the world in which you currently reside. The basic question becomes, then, how do I get there from here? How can I trust this to be real? Good questions. After all, everything about the world in which you've chosen to live seems very hard and fixed, and not at all capable of the kind of change that we are discussing here. So this discourse that we are offering to you may strike you as some kind of fanciful tale, designed to woo you into thinking that things are possible that you know simply are not.

As we enter a metaphysical discourse of this nature, we have found that the attitude of most human beings is that they will tend to believe what we speak only after we have proven something to them. Now, we know that there is nothing to prove -- and we tell them so. But we offer them an opportunity anyway to prove it to themselves. Indeed, in every case where human beings allow, the proof does come that all we have spoken of is true. And yet, humans will very often then say, well, that was interesting, but it is not enough!

Even if human beings begin to trust that all we speak is true, their greatest fear then becomes: What will others think? And further, if I do agree and allow these new ideas to become actualized within me, what will happen to all that is around me

: ◆ ◆ :

now? Will I lose the life I have? Will I lose all that I love about my current universe? These are all good questions, beloved children.

Let us begin by stating very clearly that it is not the world around you that does the changing first, it is *you* who will change, and as you do so, your universe simply must follow along. It must, for you are at the center of all and everything that you have co-created, and so it is *you* who will change, and your universe then will change with you.

We will tell you something even more useful: *If you are reading this publication, then the change has already begun.* That statement may leave you with much to think about. And that is exactly what we would ask you to do in this moment. *Sit and be still*, dear friends, and allow that which we have just spoken to begin to become a very real concept in your mind. You will see that we do not have to prove anything to you. You already know that your life is changing, and that which once tormented you is losing its sting as you allow more Light into your universe. This is so, and you know it to be so. The human mind, however, must explore all these words on these pages and have its day, as well. That is why we have presented this discourse.

Let us tell you something else, dear friends: Leia writes these words more for her own benefit than for that of anyone who may choose to read them. Even though she knows her universe has become more wondrous and joyful than she could ever have imagined in her past, it is still such an amazing phenomenon for her to accept that she must continue to come to us and ask for further support on her journey to her Light. We have been a conscious part of Leia's existence in this lifetime for more than

: ◆ ◆ :

20 years now, and still she comes to us for support in realizing the wondrous world in which she has now chosen to reside.

This brings us to another point that you may wish to know, as well. *You do not do this alone.* There is support available from the beings of Light and, most important, from your own Totality (or Higher Self) to aid you on this journey to your Light. Again, if you are reading this publication, on some level you already know this to be true. And so, dear friends, while you sit and are still, allow these beings to help you know this to be true. No, dear friends, you are not now nor have you ever been alone. To realize more consciously than ever before that this is so is one of the most profound aspects of allowing your universe to accept the attributes of the fourth dimension. As you allow it, the proof of the power of this Light to carry you into this new dimension will come. It will come. Again, the most crucial factor will be your willingness to allow it to be so. As you sit and are still and allow, it will happen. Be open and be willing, and it will happen.

Will this take you away from all that you have known and loved? Will it separate you from the universe you have always known? To be frank, that is simply impossible. The Light cannot separate, it can only include. Thus, all that you have ever been, or ever will be, will always be part of your universe. What changes is how you choose to experience this universe. As this changes within you, all that has been disharmonious, stressful and painful must also change. But your universe can never lose what you love. As you open to the loving Light of this new dimension, it can only enhance your ability to love all that is in your universe.

: ◆ ◆ :

How You Co-Create Your Universe

First, let us explain why we consistently speak of "*co*-creation." Nothing in your universe can happen without your Light. Your Light works with you to co-create consciously all that you choose to experience in your universe. This may appear to be a difficult concept to embrace with your human mind, because of its implications. First, it means that you are not a victim of your circumstances. This is a truth. *You are not a victim*, in any way whatsoever, of anything that you experience. Second, it means that you cannot blame another for your unhappiness. This is also a truth, although it flies in the face of all that human beings may wish to believe about the circumstances of their lives. Be aware that any thoughts of being a victim of circumstances, or of blaming others for what you have experienced, leave you completely disempowered to create change in your lives. Those assumptions are simply not the reality that we invite you to embrace at this time.

Some of you may also assume that it is "God's providence" that provides the circumstances of your lives and, in truth, that assumption would come closer to a true understanding of the situation. But it is not quite there yet. First, let us briefly talk about the concept of "God." This term can imply many ideas given to you by the religion of your choice. Indeed, any and all religions are giving you ideas that can help you understand that concept. However, while the same grain of truth has seeded all major world religions, the organizations that have then formed around this grain of truth have sought to disempower you and

: ♦ ♦ :

become the indispensable vehicle through which you must pass in order to know the power of your Light. For the sake of this discourse, we are asking you to consider setting aside any of the names that you have learned to describe your God, be they Allah, Buddha, Brahma, or any other term. Instead, we would like to suggest calling that which fills your being and co-creates your universe simply the "Light."

How do you co-create the universe in which you choose to reside? Let us attempt an explanation as best as possible in human terms. Your hands, which are holding this publication, your eyes, which are reading it, and the book itself are all composed of Light. *All that you perceive is Light.* Not surprisingly, your scientists have come to the same understanding. They have taken the atom and reduced it to very small particles, and have noticed that when these particles are not observed, they do not exhibit life. When they are observed, however, the particles become animated. (One of the world's great religions, Buddhism, discussed this awareness many centuries ago.) If something is not observed, it does not exist in your universe. Your scientists have called these studies quantum physics. We call it the truth that we bring to you today.

Your observation, or focus if you will, creates animation, or life in your universe. It is crucial to understand, furthermore, that your thoughts have the same effect. Since this is essential information for you to comprehend, we will repeat and emphasize this point for you: *Every thought that you think has a corresponding effect in your universe which you are co-creating in every moment.*

We ask you to think about this for a moment. For instance, have you noticed that if you meet a person and decide that you do not

: ♦ ♦ :

like that person, he or she invariably responds in kind? Have you noticed that when you think of a friend or loved one, that person may attempt to contact you, stating that he or she was thinking of you? Have you noticed that before you begin a project, you will think about it first and then bring it into manifestation on the Earth plane?

Have you further noticed that human beings have a penchant for "prophecy"? You may prophesy, for instance, that your adolescent child will not return home when promised, or would not clean his or her room as agreed upon, or would leave a mess once again? You often make predictions or pass judgment on your universe, and then find yourself correct in all these cases, and feel very smart for being so correct. Have you noticed that those predictions or judgments are frequently quite negative in nature -- which would then prove, once again, that you are living in quite a mess which, you believe, is not of your making?

What we have just described is how you tend to use the power of your Light to unwittingly co-create the universe with your very thoughts and focus. The above are just a few examples of how you have done this. Now you might wish to know how you can positively and intentionally co-create the world in which you reside.

The truth that you co-create your universe with your thoughts is most difficult for human beings to comprehend. One of the reasons is that you simply do not realize that what you have thought in the past has co-created what you are experiencing now, nor do you realize that what you are currently thinking will co-create your experiences a moment from now. Is this not so, beloved children?

: ♦ ♦ :

You need to take into consideration that, prior to incarnating in human form, you had thoughts of what you would choose to co-create in this lifetime, and those very thoughts have left you with the life-situation that you find yourself in at this time. What we are saying is that, prior to your birth, you chose your parents, your economic, political and religious experiences, your state of health, your sexual experiences and, if applicable, whom you would ultimately choose to marry -- even the circumstances of all these life events, including the birth of your children.

This statement may be perceived as contradicting the concept of freedom of choice that humans have in co-creating their universe. In fact, it may be interpreted to mean that one's whole life has already been set in stone, so to speak. Let us then mention two other widely held concepts, the ideas of "predestination" and "karma." In the history of human thinking, those ideas are indeed directly related to what we speak of now. Many religious teachings have stated quite boldly that how you lead your life now will indeed directly determine what the circumstances of your next life will be. This is the essence of the concept of "karma"; what we stated above regarding all the choices you have determined before birth -- such as whom your parents, your spouse, or your children will be -- corresponds to the concept of "karmic agreements."

What may appear confusing to you is the notion that not only have you chosen the circumstances of your life -- even those that include hardship and suffering -- but that you did this with the help of your Light, which, by definition, is only beneficent. Indeed, many who subscribe to the idea of karma believe that it is some kind of punishment for bad behavior in another lifetime,

: ◆ ◆ :

and that it is not you who would choose adversity or hardship, but "God" who would decree that you must now suffer in payment for what you have done before. Beloved children, this misconception is another way various religions have exercised control over humanity.

For the sake of this discourse, we presuppose that you have already entertained the concepts of reincarnation and karma. We will tell you, however, that what you have learned or read regarding such has only been partially accurate. In truth, beloved children, *with your human minds you cannot completely comprehend all the reasons why you have chosen any experience in this lifetime.* Your minds are simply not capable of understanding these concepts as fully as you might wish. That is why religions have sought to simplify these matters and harness them as reasons why you should behave and follow the precepts of one religion or another. Rules and regulations have come into play to continue to remind you that you have been bad and unworthy, and in need of a restrictive structure to help you finally stay good in this lifetime.

All of these notions may have been useful in the past, but as your planet enters the force field of the fourth dimension, these ideas no longer apply, and it is time for you to understand consciously more than you've ever been able to understand -- and then to apply this information to your life, so that you can move into a new way of being, in conscious concert with your Light.

Fundamentally, we wish you to understand that the only one who has chosen your karma is your Totality (or as you may call it, your Higher Self). Let us remind you once again that you have chosen to live on a plane of freewill choice. This means

: ♦ ♦ :

that the Light that informs your being is here to aid you in co-creating, through your own Totality, whatever will bring you closer to your Light. In other words, you have the freedom to choose your path. But the path you choose, as you plan your life prior to birth, will be designed for one reason only: *to bring you* ✸ *closer to your Light.*

What is the nature of this Light? It is benevolent, beneficent, all knowing, kind and wise; most important, it is unconditionally loving of all and everything. Because this Light is unconditionally loving, it has given all of creation as you know it the freedom to co-create itself with the help of this Light. What you see around you now is the direct result of that freedom.

Understand that, with the help of this Light, you can bring all that you see to a place of being benevolent, beneficent, all knowing, kind and wise. The Light can only be unconditionally loving. It cannot be unkind or seek to harm you. That is not possible. What you see in your world now that is so unpleasant was co-created by humanity using its power of free will. Now more than ever, each human being has the power to co-create a new universe that can be in keeping with the attributes of your Light. You can live in a kind and loving world -- *if you choose.*

The Earth is Awakening with You

This universe, which you may now choose to co-create with the help of your Light, will be in accordance with the direction in which your whole planet is heading. Your planet is changing frequency, dear friends, and it is moving further into its Light. The Earth is currently moving into the fourth dimension. But it will move further still -- and fairly soon, in your Earth years -- to even higher frequencies.

What you need to understand is that all the evidence that you have accumulated, in lifetime after lifetime, about this Earth -- as you remember it -- no longer applies to what we speak of now. Your Earth is changing and awakening, and its history and your history are changing and becoming accessible to the scrutiny of these new frequencies of Light. *All that has been* ✶ *will never be the same again.* This is what we ask you to know as truth.

The reason that you have chosen to be alive at this time is simple: to move with your planet to the new frequencies that are already available, or which will become more easily available in the near future. It is an exciting and wondrous experience that you have chosen. What could be more wonderful than having a human form and experiencing this glorious planet while fully awakened? What could be more joyous than residing in a universe that is moving ever more rapidly into the higher frequencies of Light that are becoming available on your glorious planet?

This is what you have chosen. In the core of your being, you know it to be true. You are reading this publication to become aware of how to do this very thing. You just need to remember what you have always known: that you are Light, and that as a sovereign being of Light, you can choose to live in harmony, balance and joy in this glorious Light, on this glorious Earth.

: ◆ ◆ :

While you may accept the statements we have put forth so far, it may be beyond your wildest imaginings -- how you can possibly change your universe, when everything you have ever known or understood about your life tells you that this is impossible. You may have accepted that you cannot push the river and that you cannot make others bend to your desires and will, that things simply are what they are and you must learn to accept the world as it is. In the past, that may have all been very, very true indeed. But now none of it is true any longer.

Now it is time for everyone to know what your great sages have always known: You carry great and powerful Light within you. Every one of you. Now it is time to awaken to that awareness and begin to use that Light, so that your universe can align to your planet's experience and you can live in harmony, balance and joy, now and for all time.

What you see around you as the escalation of suffering on your globe results from the majority of humanity struggling to hold onto the precepts of the third dimension. These precepts no longer apply. Clinging to how things have been will never bring harmony and balance or joy into anyone's life. Let us illustrate this point with an example: Someone you loved dearly left your side, either through death or other unfortunate circumstances. What happens if you seek to hold onto the energy of that person as he or she was when that person was by your side? Is it possible? Would it be enjoyable? Would it not actually lead to a form of madness to endeavor such? Beloved children, that is what you are witnessing on your planet at this time. Human beings who believe that the world as it was in the past must continue to be so in the present and the future are seeking to control and manipulate humanity to conform to these obsolete

: ◆ ◆ :

standards. Inevitably, it is painful for the human beings who endeavor to stay in these old archetypes and paradigms.

For those who wish to know this, it is now time to awaken to the realization that you can live in a different universe. Right now. These are the steps that are crucial in creating this experience for you:

- Believe, trust and expect this to be possible.
- Understand that this Light empowers you to change your universe.
- Be willing to sit with your Light on a frequent and regular basis, and allow it to work with you. As you sit, consciously surrender to your Light.
- Allow the Light to heal your being in the places where you have held fear and anger. Fear and anger block the Light from flowing freely throughout your being. When you allow the Light to heal you, it can flow even more strongly throughout your being.
- Be willing to open your heart to your Light, and allow the Light of your Totality (or Higher Self) to guide you *in every moment and in everything you do.*
- Let go of judgment of self and others in all regards. Judgment disempowers you and blocks your Light.
- Let go of trying to change the world around you. Remember, it is not broken and it does not need fixing. Everyone lives in a universe of his or her choosing, and all you can do is honor this.

Your task, beloved children, becomes to open to a new way of being. And in so doing, you will automatically change the universe in which you reside. Healing self will take you from

:♦ ♦:

your problems, fears, worries and pain. When you are no longer encumbered by such, your universe must heal with you. We will explain more on the following pages. Be patient. You will understand.

Believe, Trust and Expect What is Possible

When Leia works with other human beings to help them help themselves, she often finds that one of their major issues centers around trust. In fact, Leia has wrestled with this issue frequently with the beings of Light and with her own Higher Self. Yet, she has agreed to allow us to come through her in this discourse on trust. Having consciously collaborated with the beings of Light for over 20 years now, she has learned that there are many reasons to trust that we speak the truth. Although Leia has personally experienced many phenomena that would aid her in developing trust in the Light and the beings of Light, what she finds the most useful reason for trusting is the fact that her life has become quite joyful and continues to be so, when she follows the precepts presented here. So, the message that she personally wishes to share with all who read this publication is that the frequencies of the fourth dimension have placed her in a joyful universe filled with peace, balance and harmony -- when she allows it.

This does not mean, however, that she has turned a blind eye or a deaf ear to the choices of the human beings around her, or that she never finds herself focused on the suffering that abounds upon this planet. That is not at all true. She is probably more alert and aware than ever before of all that surrounds her. As

: ◆ ◆ :

you open to your Light -- and if you consciously choose to stay within your body as you do so -- you will find that you do become more alert and aware of the Light and all that is manifest in creation. As a consequence, you see and know more clearly all that comes into your universe. With the aid of your Light, you understand more deeply than with your human mind alone all the reasons why what you are observing has chosen to manifest in your universe. If suffering or pain becomes the focus of your awareness, you habitually breathe the Light and invoke it in response -- because you trust that the Light can heal, transmute, transform and bring into balance all that you observe.

The habit of invoking the Light is based on the understanding that, as a powerful being of Light residing in the center of your universe, you co-create by choice what happens in your universe. If you trust that the Light is an effective tool in this process of co-creation -- and how could it not be, if all that you observe comes from the Light? -- then you always invoke the Light in response to everything that comes into your universe. Everything. Every event, every being, every feeling, every thought, every awareness. All are co-created by the Light and therefore subject to invocation by you to continue to bring all within your universe into balance, harmony and joy.

What we speak of here applies to *any* example that would come to mind. For instance, let us say that you and a dearly beloved friend have fallen from grace with one another. You are now beginning to wonder what you ever saw in this human being that was so appealing and you are sure that you no longer wish to be in connection ever again. This human being has hurt your feelings deeply, and the pain that you feel cannot be denied. Now, as you co-create your universe, you may choose a series

: ◆ ◆ :

of responses that have been your pattern probably for more than one lifetime. First, you may feel angry and hurt, and may even shed a few tears. Then you may choose any number of ways to retaliate, ranging from angry words towards that human being to angry words to others regarding that human. The sentences that you speak are likely to be filled with words of judgment regarding that human being -- and such diatribes may go on for some time. If you are not prone to expressing your feelings and if you choose a silent path instead, you may withdraw from this human being; however, the hurt and angry feelings that were generated by this experience will continue for some time.

Whatever you may have chosen to do, you will realize that none of your responses have improved how you feel or what you think of the universe in which you live. Indeed, this experience has probably colored how you feel about life in general. Subsequently, you may even choose to deepen your suffering by engaging in an addictive pattern to numb your sorrow, a pattern that may include mind-altering substances, food, entertainments of many sorts, or compulsive behaviors. Once you have realized that none of this has helped you feel better, you may then decide that "time heals all wounds" -- and leave it at that.

Let us propose a more productive response, if we may. Again, remember a time when a friend has betrayed your trust in one way or another -- you may not need to go far to remember such an event in your life. If you chose any of the response patterns mentioned above, the memory will indeed still reverberate within you, for it was never healed. Assuming that the pain and anger around that experience are still within you, we would like to offer a new course of action: Sit and be still; begin to breathe slowly and deeply, and invoke the presence of the Light to

: ♦ ♦ :

come to you and fill you with each breath in. As you breathe, you may ask your heart to open to this Light, while you allow yourself to feel the pain and anger. Just feel it. Then you may ask the Light to help you feel compassion and unconditional love for self, as you go through the pain of the experience. Ask the Light to help you heal your pain and *trust* that this will be so. *Trust*, dear friends, and expect that your heart will heal from the pain of the experience.

In truth, that is all you need do. All the other activities that you have tried before never led you to what you truly wanted, after you first felt the pain. All you really wanted was to heal the pain. Nothing you tried accomplished that. But the Light will heal the pain. It must, for it is unconditional love, and when you allow it to do so, it will lovingly help you heal your pain. As you begin to feel this healing, you will start to feel compassion for self, and you will find that compassion begins to develop within you for the human being who behaved in such a "terrible" way toward you. As your heart heals, and as you listen to the wisdom that the Light has to offer, you will understand that invariably it was suffering and confusion that caused the other person to exhibit the uncomfortable behavior in the first place. That is indeed a profound insight.

In time, then, you will find that the sting is gone. The pain is gone, and you are feeling nurtured by the Light which loves you. Your universe has returned to balance, harmony and joy. You may or may not wish to continue to be in relationship with the human being who was the catalyst for this experience, but you will know that your heart can now be at peace. This is what Leia has come to trust.

: ♦ ♦ :

Understand That the Light Empowers You to Change Your Universe

Beloved children, you are Light. It courses through your veins and arteries, and fills every part of your body. This is the same for all you behold. It is everywhere and in everything. It would be true to say that Light is the "matter" that builds your universe. Where does this Light come from? That question has filled volumes of religious treatises and caused great discussion, debate, and even wars upon your human plane. So far, we have not even discussed the nature of this Light. We only ask here: Where does it come from? And already, we could be at war with various factions of humanity. But we shall answer this question anyway. The Light comes from Infinite Source. Then you may ask: "What is Infinite Source?" It is the Source of All and Everything. Some may choose to call this God, some call it Brahma, some call it Allah. In truth, the name does not matter. It goes beyond the limitation of title. It simply *is,* and it is everywhere in your universe, represented by the Light that you behold in everything, including yourselves.

Now we ask: What is the nature of this Light? The answer, in truth, is simple: It is all-knowing, all-loving, kind and nurturing to all that exists in its creation. Just as a mother and father would love their child and only wish the very best for that child, so does the Light love you. Then you may ask, if this is so, why am I suffering on this Earth? Again we answer as we have so often. Infinite Source has created a plane of freewill choice, where you may co-create whatever you wish to experience -- and that is what you have done.

:◆:

This truth may go against all that you have come to believe in this and other lifetimes. You have been taught to believe that "things happen to you" and, indeed, you have often ascribed painful events to the very "God" that we now tell you is the Infinite Source of benevolent, loving Light. You have also been taught to believe that you must fulfill certain criteria or be a certain way to deserve the love of this God. This is not so. Infinite Source loves you already, with the Light that animates your body. This may be difficult for you to accept and understand. But it is true. You have chosen to be alive now to *know* that this is true. For it is easier than ever before to experience the essence of this loving Light -- and *it will only become easier, as time passes on your plane.*

Again, all that we ask of you is to sit and be still, and allow a conscious awareness of the Light. Meditate quietly, and simply allow your focus to be with the Light that is already in you. Feel it in your heart, and allow it to tell you how it loves you. Leia and Manalus have allowed this for themselves, and they have helped many others to know it and feel it, as well. This Light simply loves you. If you are still and call to it, it will reveal itself to you.

If you listen to the omniscient Light within, it will help you to know how you can co-create your universe in new ways that will bring it into balance, harmony and joy. The Light,, which guides all that you see with its radiance, not only wants your trees, plants and creatures to be healthy, strong and beautiful, it wishes the same for *all* of creation, and that includes you. Because of your history, you fight this natural flow of loving Light. When you allow your history to fall away, you leave yourself open to being loved and nurtured by your Light. You, too, can be healthy, strong, beautiful and at peace in your

: ◆ ◆ :

universe. That is what is happening to your whole planet now, and you are asked to join in co-creating this natural order. *Let your history remain your history. It need no longer apply in your present or in your future.* Open now to let this Light love you and care for you unconditionally. All you need do is open to it and acknowledge that it is there. This is not a fairy tale, children; this is truth.

Sit and Be Still as Frequently as Possible, and Surrender to Your Light

Perhaps you may say to us, "Master, I do sit, and I am still, and I don't really find that much happens or if I do, I don't exactly see how this will change my universe and bring me into the fourth dimension of peace, balance and joy." And now we come to the crux of the matter. All that we have spoken of before is perhaps not as useful for you as this particular bit of information: *If you don't allow the Light to help you, then it cannot.*

"ALLOWING"

Often we see humans sit and endeavor to be still, and wait, and wait, and wait for something to happen to them that will make them feel better, or help them with their lives -- and yet they say that nothing ever really improves their lives. They still suffer and feel unhappy, and are waiting for that something wonderful to happen that will make everything okay. And they try many things that they believe might make them feel better -- but nothing ever does. They may say, "Well, if I didn't have to deal with all those people in my universe who are unpleasant, then perhaps I would be happier. Or if I had more money or felt

: ◆ ◆ :

better about my health and my body, then I would be happier. Or if I had more strength and energy, then I would feel better. Or if world events were more pleasant, then I would be happier. Or if there was someone to love me as I wish to be loved, then I would feel better." Or they may say, "Okay, I do feel better when I sit with my Light, but then I must go back into my universe where I am still unhappy and things still aren't right, and I still don't see how sitting with my Light changes any of that. Bad things still happen."

There are two points to notice about all these statements. Either the statements contain the words "if" and "then," or they contain the word "but." This means that the humans are sitting with their Light on a conditional basis. They want the Light to prove itself to them. In other words, if they sit with the Light, then the Light must fix up their lives in response. They know how they want their lives to be fixed up. They are still focusing on their problems, anticipating new problems, and gleefully proving themselves correct in how those problems arise and remain prevalent within their lives. They mistakenly assume that the Light must fix these problems, and when they go back and check, they find that the sitting didn't help with any of that at all.

Beloved children, sitting isn't enough. The rest of the directive involves the act of *surrender*. And therein lies the rub. You don't know how to do that. And if you did understand how to do that, you wouldn't actually want to do that. In most human beings' understanding, surrender means "to give away your power." Your life already appears to be an exercise in giving away your power, and you've had enough of that. That is why, when you sit with your Light, you have in place a list of demands as to how you think things ought to change for the

: ◆ ◆ :

better. When those things don't happen, it is proof that the Light doesn't work. Be aware that you haven't given the Light a chance to do its work. If you don't surrender to it, you never will.

Let us review some of the properties of the Light that we have already mentioned. The Light that flows through you is omniscient. What does that mean? It is all-knowing. Can you say that about your human mind? In your life so far, have you found that your human mind has had all the answers and that it has been correct every time? We assume not. Beloved children, you *do* have something at your disposal that does have all the answers -- and is correct every time. We are asking you to trust this. Yes, children, *surrender* to this. The Light *does* have all the answers.

Another property of the Light is that it loves you unconditionally. Its purpose is to take care of you. Now, with your human mind you may think you know what that means. It's supposed to fix all your problems. And you know what those problems are. You don't so much sit with your Light as sit *in expectation* of what your Light ought to be doing for you. Instead, we ask you to sit with your Light and *surrender* to it. Allow it to guide you. It knows what to do. Have you given it a chance to guide you? We can't make you do this. The Light can't make you do this. Only *you* can surrender. You can invoke the Light with your conscious will and affirm that you surrender to its loving, omniscient wisdom -- and then get out of the way and let it help you. It will show you what to do. It will guide you. Sit and be still, and let it help you. The Light is here to help you in every moment. Breathe the Light as you move through your day. Stop, be still, and listen. This is more easily accomplished than ever before. Remember, you are not alone.

: ♦ ♦ :

There is help in every moment. Allow yourself to be loved and cared for. *Surrender* to your Light. Allow it to guide you through every part of your existence. You will see. You will see.

Allow the Light to Heal your Fear and Anger

Now, beloved children, we come to the place where it appears that you have much work to do, for you have all lived many, many lifetimes on your Earth plane, and these have not always been the most enjoyable experiences. Each time you have experienced pain in other lifetimes, it has always been caused by fear and anger. You have kept the memory of those feelings within you from one lifetime to the next.

When you then try to consider how you could possibly retain memories from each and every episode from each and every lifetime, this may appear a bit mind-boggling. Here is another, even more interesting thought that can aid you in understanding. You have always had only one reason for being: to be fully connected to the Light of Source in every moment. And all the experiences you have ever chosen have been chosen by you to bring you to that full connection with the Light.

As you embodied in this lifetime, you once again set up the circumstances of your birth, youth and all you have experienced to this time to mimic the most profound experiences of other lifetimes that have been most challenging in keeping you from your Light.

: ♦ ♦ :

That is why so many of you have found this particular lifetime so very uncomfortable and thus have bemoaned your choice of embodiment ("What was I thinking?").

Instead of seeing this life as being such a bad time for you, we ask you to consider it a time of extraordinary opportunity, when you can experience significant growth and healing more easily than ever before. Your life has been perfectly designed to aid you in this. Let go of your sorrow and begin to see what is now possible for you. In actuality, you have chosen to be alive in the circumstances in which you find yourself so that you can easily realize what you wish to heal in your being -- issues you have chosen to experience in many, many lifetimes. Dealing with your issues using the tools of awareness gained in this lifetime allows you to carry the Light of Source more fully within your form than has ever been possible in any other lifetime *since time began.*

It is a wondrous time to be alive, beloved children, and to be able to see so clearly what you wish to heal within self as you move into full empowerment with your Light. This is absolutely possible now. The fact that you are reading these pages means that this is what you wish to do. And you can.

You may ask, "How can I realize what I wish to heal?" The answer is simple. If you are uncomfortable with *any* area of your life, then that is what you wish to heal. As soon as you find yourself in *any* discomfort, be it pain, sadness, anger or fear, give yourself the grace of sitting still and asking yourself: "What is the source of my discomfort?" Your first response will probably be to blame yourself and/or whoever is closest to you. What you are coming to is a conclusion that simply shows your confusion. But we would ask you to keep looking. Go within,

: ♦ ♦ :

and see where the pain lies within your body. It is probably in or around your heart, for that is where the Light is strongest in your being, and it can easily show where the pain resides. The uncomfortable feeling may have words, thoughts or pictures attached to it. Leia and Manalus have produced books that describe the healing process in greater detail. But for now, we ask you to trust that what you perceive as painful within can be alleviated.

Even if you wish to remain angry or fearful -- and that would never be judged by the beings of Light -- even if your conscious mind wishes to cling to your suffering, you can nevertheless sit and be still, call in the Light and ask for help in healing. The healing will come, beloved friends.

As you allow this healing, you will understand that all has been designed -- and indeed is in perfect order -- for you to come closer to your Light and consciously allow it to fill your being. You will come to realize a wonderful perfection to all you have co-created in this and every other lifetime. No, beloved children, none of it has been a mistake. Thinking that you made mistakes is only an outgrowth of your ego-mind choosing to punish you. The Light can only love you and is here to help you know this to be true. Allow it, and you will see. This Light can bring you the balance, harmony and joy that you seek in your universe.

: ♦ ♦ :

Allow the Light to Guide You in Every Moment and in Everything You Do

We have discussed how you can heal the fears within your being. Now we discuss a need for a conscious willingness on your part to allow the Light to fill your being and guide you in all that you do. This may sound simple indeed. But we have observed that most human beings find this to be the hardest thing to do.

You all wish to be well. We have not heard otherwise from any of you. But few, if any, really wish to relinquish the control of your human minds over your being and allow this Light to carry you forth in all affairs. You all agree that things are not as you would wish them to be, but you haven't quite given up the notion that somehow your human mind will figure out a way to make things right. We have found that this usually involves your human mind seeking to manipulate, control and respond in a less than advantageous manner to any and all situations -- although at the time of any given ego-mind response, you are convinced that everything should turn out all right this time. In actuality, however, you are continuously disappointed by the results. Time and again, your problems have not dissipated, and disappointment is the result. With great regularity, this is the outcome of your mental machinations. Even after you have worried, stewed, fretted, complained, discussed and rationalized any given situation, you still find that discomfort, disappointment, pain and suffering remain the order of the day.

Yet, when we say to you, there is another way that is foolproof -- and do not take that term lightly -- you respond, "It sounds good, but if it involves relinquishing the power of my human

: ♦ ♦ :

mind to anything else, even if it is my own Higher Self, forget it. I simply can't do it." And this is truth. You can't or, in many cases, you simply won't. This statement may sound shocking, coming from your friends, the beings of Light, but to this time, this has been true for most of humanity.

This is one of the reasons why your planet, Mother Earth, has chosen the course of action in every area that you are currently witnessing. These events, which you may call "Earth changes," have been co-created by you, because it appears you need to experience more of what you are currently living with, before you come to believe that another way of conducting your lives will actually be more useful to you. As soon as a critical mass of humanity chooses to move to the higher frequencies and surrender guidance of their beings to their Light, the difficulties on the human plane will end. This shift will happen one human at a time.

It is now easier than ever before for you to move to the higher frequencies and allow them to guide you in your life. As the frequencies of your planet continue to change, this can only be increasingly so. Conversely, if you choose to try to remain as you are now, the third dimensional frequencies that work with your human mind will feel ever more uncomfortable. Why is this so?

The reason is simple. When you have opened for even a glimpse of the higher frequencies -- in meditation and in other ways -- this has felt more wonderful than ever before. Thus, when you return to a third dimensional way of being, the disparity is greater. We have often said, where there is more Light, there is more shadow. Beloved friends, there is more Light than ever before on your human plane! Therefore, the

: ◆ ◆ :

shadow is greater, the disparity is more apparent and thus it is more uncomfortable, when you try to remain as you have been in the past.

The past is dissolving, beloved friends, as are all the paradigms that you have lived with to this time. As we have mentioned previously in this publication, this is easy for you to see -- if you choose to acknowledge it. When you endeavor to cling to ways of being that you have always known, the discomfort therefore can only increase.

Sooner or later, you may finally wish to try a new way of being. This new way of being will immerse you in the frequencies of what you now call the fourth dimension, and it will open you to accepting the higher frequencies that are still to come on your planet. So, how can you do this? How can you open your heart to the Light of Source within and allow it to guide your conscious mind?

It is far easier than you might wish to believe. But it does require *discipline* and *mindfulness*. *Discipline* to sit and be still each day, and invite the Light of your Higher Self to take up full residence in the wheel of Light at your heart -- and *mindfulness* to continually keep an awareness that, although your mind wishes to dictate all your actions, you now choose the Light in your heart to fill your mind and guide it *in everything you do*.

This may sound surprising to you, if you believe that your Light only deals with "spiritual" matters. But your Light is competent and prepared to deal with much more than that particular area. Remember, your Higher Self is all-knowing, omniscient. It is compassionate and wise beyond all measure. When your human mind does not have the answer to even the most trivial question,

: ♦ ♦ :

we can assure you emphatically, your Higher Self will have the answer.

All that is required of you is to sit and be still, and allow this omniscience to guide you. As you develop the discipline to listen and allow the Light to guide you, you will see that its wisdom will lead you out of the confusion, pain, and suffering in which you are currently choosing to reside. *This Light has the answer to everything you have ever wished to know. It has the solution to every problem.* If you simply listen, it will tell you all. If you follow the guidance, your universe will change, and you will become joyfully fulfilled within the realm of the fourth dimension and in the beauty of the Light that is within all and everything. Your eyes will open, your heart will be open, and your being will be at peace, joyfully experiencing the universe that you have co-created.

Up to this time, it has not been easy for you to do what we propose. But it is easier now than ever before. And when you choose suffering, know that in an instant you can open your heart and listen in order to know, in every single moment, what you can do to regain the loving Light of Source within your heart and your world. Trust what you hear, for it only speaks loving words to you that will ease your suffering. If other words come to your mind that would propose any course of action that could cause suffering for you or others, know that your human mind is still in play; sit again and ask for the Light. It is with you always. Listen, and you will know it. It can be done, beloved children. It can be done.

: ◆ ◆ :

Let Go of Judgment of Self and Others
in All Things

The above appears to be a simple statement that is easily understood by one and all. However, even if in this very moment you were to say to us that you agree with what we suggest here and will no longer judge, you will find that within the next hour you will have judged yourself, a particular situation, or another. You may have come to a conclusion, or you may have observed something and had an opinion. Or you will have done something that you do habitually, and that is to evaluate your own performance in a given situation. And when you choose to do any of these things, beloved friends, you have judged.

So you may come to the conclusion that this appears more difficult than you first imagined -- and we would absolutely agree. It is. Your ego-mind has had centuries to develop these attributes and only a few moments, in the scheme of all things, to let them go. But we encourage you to do so, and here is why: *When you judge, in truth, you do nothing but harm yourself in many, many ways.*

Let us give you some examples of how human beings engage in judgment.

You are walking along a crowded street. Is it not true, beloved children, that when you observe other human beings, as you may very casually do while walking along, that you judge and evaluate the appearance of them? If you say you do not, then you are a rare person indeed. Let us say, then, that you see people who are of a different class than you. What comes to

: ♦ ♦ :

your conscious mind? Would you wish to spend time with someone who appears less financially capable of caring for him or herself than you are? Let us suppose the person is of a different skin tone, or wears clothes that are foreign to you. Would that encourage or discourage your desire to associate with that person? Further, let us say that a person does not weigh a "respectable" amount. In your culture, this is common, but quite frowned upon, isn't it? Furthermore, a person may come by who is doing something rude, in relation to the other humans around him or her. Would you wish to associate with that person? Perhaps he or she is mentally disturbed or using a mind-altering substance. Would this person have your approval? Or would you wish to judge those as poor behaviors? And then you observe the traffic, and someone drives poorly and causes others some difficulty, as a result. What would you think of this situation?

Let us continue the scenario: You have returned to your home and are now preparing to go out into society for an evening with your friends that promises to be great fun. However, when you stand before the mirror, you realize that your attire may be incorrect and be subject to a poor reception by others at the gathering. Furthermore, it comes to your attention that your shoes appear old and you have no new ones to replace them. In addition, you realize that you weigh more than you wish and the only clothes you think you can wear make you look even heavier. You come to the conclusion that the only thing to do is cancel your evening, because you can't bear to be seen as you now perceive yourself. Nevertheless, you go ahead anyway and leave your home, and get behind the wheel of your automobile. Since you are so overwrought at the thought of how others may perceive you, you do not pay attention to your driving and

: ♦ ♦ :

consequently cause an accident, thereby ending any thoughts of an enjoyable evening with friends.

You see, beloved children, *when you choose to judge another, all that happens is that you create a universe in which you live in fear of being judged by others yourself.* Because of the power of the Light you now carry, you invariably attract to you that which you most fear. This "mechanism" is only growing stronger with time. What you fear, you will quickly bring to self -- more quickly now than ever before. Thus, when you judge another, realize that you will also fear, and rightly so, that the same judgment will come to you. Again, we do not ordain this; it is karmic law. You co-create this with your own Higher Self.

Why would that be so? Every experience you choose is for one reason only: to bring you closer to your Light. And if you choose to judge anyone or anything, your own Light will offer you the opportunity to experience what you have judged, so that you may have the opportunity to heal the fears underlying your judgment.

Judgment is one of the favorite pastimes of humanity. What can you do instead of judging? How can you occupy your mind instead? The answer is simple. It is a given that your mind will continue to choose this activity. You will always carry with you everything that you have always been, so we do not say that by tomorrow you will have lost the ability to judge anything. You won't. But you can choose to follow the judgment that comes to your mind with a very simple act: *You can breathe the Light through your heart each time you sense a judgment in your mind.* That is all we ask you to do. That is all.

: ◆ ◆ :

When you do this, you will begin to notice two things happening. First, you will notice that all that you have judged is illusory. It is not real. It is just what you are observing in your world to which you then decide to assign a certain value as good or bad. It is simply a trick your mind plays, based on your conditioning. For instance, in some cultures, human beings who carry great physical weight are considered quite attractive, as opposed to the hard-and-fast judgment most of you have made about others who are heavy. Remember, no two human beings are alike. What you love, another may hate, and vice versa. Who is to say that your judgment regarding anything reflects the only true and right way things must be?

Second, as you breathe the Light through your heart, you will notice something else replacing your judgment. Since the Light can only be unconditionally loving and compassionate, you feel that love when you breathe the Light. You will feel love not only for the others in your universe, but for yourself as well. As you do this, you will begin to realize that *you can simply be in this Light and love others as they are.* The surprising thing you then find is that others respond in kind. When you are kind, loving and centered in your Light, you create a universe where others will respond in kind. Even if another cannot respond with kindness, you would be less willing to judge them. The compassion that this Light offers to you will let you know that it is only pain and fear that stops others from being kind.

Do you understand, beloved children? *All that you perceive is of your making.* When you cease judging, you free yourself to be your loving Light in response to all you perceive. The discomfort ceases and joy remains.

: ◆ ◆ :

Let Go of Trying to Change the World Around You

This statement may appear very confusing indeed. After all, the first question you may ask in response is why are we aiding Leia in this publication, if we are telling you not to change the world around you? Aren't we trying to do the very thing we suggest not to do? That would indeed be a very good question, given the circumstances in which you are reading this. Are we trying to change you? The answer is no, we are not. First and foremost, we are not trying to change you because we cannot. *Only you can change yourself!*

That is crucial information for you to know, and we advise you to take this information seriously. Most humans are very busily endeavoring to change everyone and everything in the world around them. This is not producing great joy in anyone -- neither the people who are endeavoring to change the world around them, nor the people who feel that someone is trying to change them. No one appears very happy with this arrangement, and rightly so. *You cannot change the world around you; you can only change yourself.*

This brings us back to the question of what are we doing here with Leia. Well, we are offering you information that you have asked to know. If you had not requested this information for yourself, you would not have procured this publication in order to find these answers.

There are only two services we can provide to you: We can offer you information and perspective that may help you

: ♦ ♦ :

understand the world you live in, and we can answer your call for help by aiding you in creating your own change. The latter we do by adding our Light to yours as you request it. But do understand, beloved children, that because you live on a plane of freewill choice, we cannot do any of these things without your request. You co-create your universe with your Light, and you co-create change in the same manner. We can help you in the two ways we have mentioned, and only in those ways.

You may say to us, "Master, this is all well and good, if you reside on the higher planes. But how about situations between human beings?" Again, we suggest to follow the same principles as those that we outlined above for our own conduct in regard to you. It is a useful way to be and actually can lead to greater harmony in every area of your world, if you would choose it.

Remember, what we speak of here is how to navigate the new frequencies that are more and more prevalent on your Earth plane at this time. In the past, you have thought that you could be effective in forcing your will upon another human being or another group of human beings, in order to create change. Indeed, much change has occurred on your human plane because of this type of behavior. However, it is not occurring with as much success as it once did. The institutions that have been put into place to force such change upon humanity are losing their power and effectiveness, and are ultimately dissolving. In the days to come, what was coerced will no longer remain -- on any level. However, the great changes that occurred not as a result of coercion but as a natural evolution in the course of humanity will remain.

: ♦ ♦ :

Any change that is forced or imposed upon another human being simply will not last. It cannot. It is in complete contradiction to the nature of the Light of Infinite Source. Since it does not have the power of the Light behind it to survive, in time it will simply fade away or fall apart. Any laws that promote unkind acts, such as acts of greed, exploitation, aggression or the imposition of force, will simply fail in their mission to subdue, subject or change humanity in any way.

The Light is loving, benevolent, kind and compassionate, and is only here to nurture life and promote well-being in humanity. As beings of Light, we are here to help you find ways to live within this Light. But we cannot do it for you. We cannot change you. You can only change yourselves. Thus, when you meet other human beings who wish to change you, thank them for their concern. Let them know that you are opening to your Light in the best way you know how, and that, although their efforts may be well meaning, you would prefer their support in finding your way for yourself.

The same would apply to you then, beloved children. We ask you to honor another's path and support him or her in finding the Light. By honoring, we mean that you will choose not to judge how another is at any given moment.

All of you, beloved children, can find your Light when you focus on yourselves and sit and are still. Then you may choose to invoke the Light to help others find their way as well. This is a fruitful, kind and benevolent act, which does not involve judgment. In your time of stillness, you may also invoke the Light for Mother Earth and all who reside upon her. The Light knows what to do to aid your planet at this time. All you need

: ♦ ♦ :

do is ask -- and then know that what you see is in perfect order for all who dwell upon your Earth. You may trust this to be so.

Open to a New Way of Being – and Thus Change the Universe in Which You Reside

Change begins within. This is completely contrary to everything you have been conditioned to believe since your earliest days in this lifetime, and indeed, in all your lifetimes in recent millennia. You have been taught to believe that the universe is an unmovable object that you must learn to cope with as best you can. You have been taught, if you haven't liked how your universe has been, to go outward and endeavor to effect change in it. What we tell you here, however, is the exact opposite of that approach.

You probably have noticed by now that any attempts you have made to change your universe as you would wish it to be have not met with much success. Furthermore, you have become aware that there are parts of your universe, as you understand it now, that would be impervious to any efforts you might make in this regard.

Given your track record in effecting change within your universe using the "old" tools that we discussed previously, we would ask you: What have you got to lose by trying another way of being? Indeed, if you try the precepts offered here, there is much to gain: peace, harmony and balance within yourselves, as well as in the universe around you.

: ♦ ♦ :

A caveat is in order, however: If you choose to do any of what we have offered here while still clinging to an agenda within your mind, you will find yourself sorely disappointed in the results. You will be disappointed, because you will have failed to surrender your expectations.

Once again, we remind you that you choose your experiences for one reason only: *to bring you closer to your Light.* If you are sitting and being still, and allowing this Light to guide you in all that you do, then you will neither have expectations nor find yourself disappointed when things don't happen as you had expected. You will trust that the Light is leading you in perfect ways that are always in your Highest Good.

You will find that this Light simply continues to guide you from moment to moment in a path of harmony and balance. It does not matter what others choose to do as they enter or leave your universe; you will be continuously counseled by this Light and therefore will only choose those actions that keep you in harmony and balance with this Light.
If someone wishing to do you harm comes into your universe, when you react with an open, loving heart instead of fear, their response must change.

Why must this be so? Because everything in your universe is energy, beloved children. It is energy infused with Light. And when you respond from your Light, then what must come back to you will also be filled with the energy infused with Light. This we ask you to trust.

With the new frequencies now available on your Earth, this is the only result possible. We know this is difficult for you to believe. Even Leia is interjecting that this is difficult for her to

: ♦ ♦ :

believe, despite the fact that she frequently uses the precepts elucidated here and has seen the beneficent results that occur when she does. She is asking: "Will the response from another who is seeking to do me harm always be from the Light?" And we ask Leia, even if another has come to her with malice, has her life in recent years improved or worsened? She must answer that it has only improved, even when she has been aware that there is someone coming to her who does not wish her well. We remind her that, when she has been aware of such a situation, she has consistently chosen to address the fears and heal them, and then to respond with love in her heart to the best of her ability. That is why her life has continued to be ever more harmonious and balanced.

Again, everything that you bring into your universe is for one reason only: *To bring you closer to your Light.* When you allow this Light to be your only response, then your universe continues to be filled with that very same Light. It is true, beloved children. It is true.

We know that, on some level, this can still be confusing to your human mind, for your mind would wish you to continue to suffer as you always have. That is all it has ever consciously known for many centuries now. But that is not the world in which you are going to reside in the days to come.

All you are being asked to do with your conscious awareness is to allow the Light to flow through you unencumbered. And you are asked to know that, as you listen to this Light, the whole planet is being drenched in these frequencies of unconditionally loving Light.
You are being asked to immerse yourself in this energy and allow your universe to change.

: ♦ ♦ :

We reiterate: If you choose to allow your ego-mind to cling to how things have been, your universe will only become more and more uncomfortable. We do not mandate this; it is simply so. Let it go, beloved children. Let it go and heal yourselves. Let the new energies of unbounded, loving Light fill your beings and your universe. Move on, children, move on.

:♦♦: :♦♦: :♦♦:

:♦♦:

The One-Percent Solution

By Martin Luthke

On the preceding pages, the Masters have implored us to break with the patterns of the past and to embrace the unique opportunities of this unprecedented time. We have heard repeatedly that a new reality is now available to one and all -- and more easily so than ever. Their valiant efforts of persuasion notwithstanding, you probably wonder whether you can do what you have never done before. The call of the Masters to enter the fourth dimension may still seem like a daunting task.

If we find that we carry a fear, in this case the fear of failure, the most useful response is one of compassion and non-judgment toward self. The second most useful response is to ask for help with healing the fear. And the third significant step is to trust that we are receiving the help for which we asked. When we are facing a daunting task, it may also be useful to break it down into smaller steps that do not seem quite so challenging.

Staying Present, Achieving Mindfulness

Energy follows consciousness. When we erect barriers of consciousness we create barriers to the flow of Light within. The Light can only guide, help and heal us to the degree that we are mindful and consciously present in our body. It works *with* us, but not *for* us. Metaphysically speaking, the Light cannot be on if nobody is home.

: ◆ ◆ :

Most of us choose a host of strategies to keep ourselves less than present, conscious or aware. It may be no exaggeration to assume that most people most of the time are "on autopilot," "sleepwalking," or "out-of-body." What are the ways that we achieve this state of mind? We choose a life full of stress, distractions, addictions and habits that *serve the purpose* of creating mindlessness and numbing of consciousness.

Why would we do that? Being alive and having a body is a mixed blessing for most of us. Within us, we carry the memories of thousands of – all too often painful -- lifetimes, our present life may be rather painful, and even if we aren't in acute pain at this time, we all are afraid of pain. In fact, it is not so much the pain itself as the *fear of pain* that motivates us to avoid awareness and to choose unconsciousness as our predominant state of mind.

Instinctively we feel that if we "avert our eyes," the pain will go away. The fact is, however, that the pain will be preserved into eternity. Why? If we withdraw consciousness, we automatically withdraw from the Light, which consequently cannot transform and transmute the pain. The prerequisite of healing is very simple: In order to heal it, you need to feel it.

Thus, it is important to stay present in one's body and to develop a mindfulness of one's actions, feelings, and thoughts. Here are some suggestions that may be helpful.

(1) Develop the discipline of taking an inventory of your thoughts, feelings and states of mind on a regular basis. Throughout the day, ask yourself: Am I present? How is my breathing? What am I feeling? Why am I doing what I am doing? Is my heart open? Am I connected to my Light? Are

: ◆ ◆ :

my thoughts nurturing and supporting me, or are they detrimental? What am I afraid of at this moment?

(2) Avoid all habits and addictions that are designed to keep you in a state of mindlessness. That may include eating foods you crave; taking mind-altering substances; using the TV, radio or computer to distract yourself thoughtlessly; seeking out numbing, mindless activities, etc.

(3) Choose activities that "get you into your body" such as gardening, physical exercise, Tai chi, etc. Allow for time with nature. "Chop wood, carry water."

(4) Develop a meditation practice that helps you become conscious of your Light while being in touch with your emotional body. Avoid a practice that is geared toward disconnecting you from your body and taking you into "lala-land."

Allowing Your Light to Love You

We put up many barriers between ourselves and our Light. We may feel unworthy and undeserving of the Light, we may feel abandoned by it, we may hold a grudge against God and the rest of life, we may be outright angry with the Light, we may fear that it may overwhelm us -- or that we may abuse it or lose it -- once we allow it in, and so on. Of course, all those barriers are based on illusion. The truth is that your Light is already within you; it is in every cell of your body, and you are made up of it. The Light is waiting patiently for you to realize this basic truth.

: ◆ ◆ :

The truth is really quite simple. The Light loves you without question, without limit, and at all times. You do not need to do anything to make that happen. There are no questions asked and no qualifications demanded. You do not need to change or to improve. There is no need to strive or to attain. The Light simply *is,* and its essence is unconditional *Love.* It is already within you, all it asks is for you to accept it. Simple, isn't it?

The One-Percent Solution

At this point, most of us may still have difficulty staying present, achieving mindfulness, and allowing our Light to love ourselves. If getting there from where you are still feels like a daunting journey, we suggest the following protocol.

Upon awakening in the morning, and throughout the day, use the following affirmations:

- "Just for today, I choose to be present and mindful. I allow my Light to fully inhabit my body."
- "Just for today, I allow my Light to love me and nurture me -- without question, reason, or limit."

Then ask your Light to help you in the process -- and trust that the help is forthcoming.

If you find yourself falling short of the stated affirmations, think of your transformation as a gradual process. Imagine that you are shifting toward mindfulness and unconditional love for self at a rate of just one percent every day. Do you think you can do that, given that the Light is in your court, offering its support

: ♦ ♦ :

eagerly? Imagine how far you could come, after a hundred days! Even if you can only approach what you affirm at the rate of one tenth of one percent per day, it would still take less than three years to transform habits that you have built up over thousands of years.

If the task of changing seems daunting, turn to the one-percent solution.

: ♦ ♦ :   : ♦ ♦ :   : ♦ ♦ :

: ♦ ♦ :

Appendix

The Ascended Masters Newsletters

The following pages contain reprints of the first ten issues of the *Ascended Masters Newsletter,* which we publish periodically via the Internet.[3] They were added to the main body of this book as a bonus.[4] While they contain many of the same ideas as those expressed on the preceding pages, we have found from our own experience that repetition does help in assimilating the new way of thinking that the Masters are proposing. After reading the main body of the book, you may choose to read one newsletter at a time to reinforce your transformation process.

Ascended Masters Newsletter # 1

Know the Power of Your Light in this Sacred Time

We thank you, beloved children, for this opportunity to be with you this day. As Leia [who gave a brief introduction] has stated, we have known all of you before this day, we have known all of you quite well indeed. All of you have experienced lifetimes with us when we walked the human plane with you. All of you

---

[3] If you wish to subscribe to this free newsletter, please send an e-mail to that effect to expansion@u-r-light.com.

[4] The newsletters are transcripts of group channeling sessions and were not edited to the same standards as the main body of the book.

have delved into the mysteries of your planet and have endeavored to understand in past lifetimes why you are here. Indeed, you have all asked that question in this lifetime, "Why am I here now?"

In each and every one of those lifetimes it was your freewill choice that brought you here. That is not always easy to understand, especially when you understand that walking the path of human life is not always pleasurable. Indeed, at this time you have entered a time on the human plane when there is great suffering -- although you have known that in every lifetime -- but the level of suffering that may come to your plane this time around may be formidable. And you are aware of this.

Each of you has asked one burning question, and that question is: *What have I agreed to do during this lifetime to alleviate the suffering on this planet?* Is that not truth, beloved children? Have you not all asked that question? What can I do in this lifetime to alleviate the suffering? What have I agreed to do? And you have asked yourselves, who am I to think that I could alleviate the suffering on this planet, especially in the face of feeling so powerless at this time? Have any of you in this gathering felt powerless given the events that you have observed in recent days? [This comment refers to the push for a war in Iraq.]

Why have you come here this day and why have we come here to be with you in conscious communication? (For, of course, we are always with you.) Why is this a time to speak words and why has Leia thought it would be important to share the knowledge that she and Manalus have received regarding the time in which you live, and what is currently occurring on your planet?

What have you noticed, children, about this time in which you live? Is there strife, is there discord, is there discontent? Are warriors arising who wish to add to the suffering on your planet? Of course, you know

:♦♦:

about such. In response you may ask, who am I to aid the suffering? What do I have to offer?

Some of you are aware that there was a "grand experiment" on your human plane. Do you know of such a thing [referring to the "experiment" initiated by James Twyman]? Human beings gathered or sat alone all over the world and prayed for harmony and balance to return to your Earth. Yesterday, and again today, human beings are gathering to speak of peace and to demonstrate for peace in large numbers. And their voices have been heard.

It appears, however, that forces are still aligned that wish to do battle. As we have said to Leia and Manalus, it appears that war is still inevitable for your human plane at this time. You may then say, "But Master, if human beings have spoken up, if human beings have sat and meditated, if human beings are trying to aid the suffering and you still say to us, for your human plane at this time war is inevitable, then how can we help? Why must we try, and indeed, why must we still wish to be alive at this time of great suffering for humanity?

At this point we ask you to entertain, if you will, a completely different understanding of your world, of your planet, and of your own lives. *We ask you to consider this time a very sacred time for your planet.* You are about to embark on a time of great cleansing and transformation for your human plane. The word that is most important for your human mind to comprehend is the word *transformation*. *Transformation begins within each one of you.*

Consider, if you will, that each being on your human plane resides within the center of his or her own universe. All who are gathered here appear to be sharing the same event, do they not? However, we ask you to honor the truth that each one of you is having your own unique experience of this event from the center of your own universe that you have co-created with your Light from your Totality (or Higher Self).

: ♦ ♦ :

Each of you is a unique being of Light, bringing to this time and space all that you have ever been or ever will be. The most important question we ask you today is: *What do you wish to co-create from the center of your universe as you reside and walk upon the human plane during this time of great challenge for all and everything of this creation?* What do you wish to be your truth in this time and space?

Are you a being of Light who has chosen a human form? Indeed, you are. What is the greatest contribution that you can give to your planet at this time? *Your greatest contribution is your Light.* For your own sake, for the sake of your universe, and for the sake of all and everything that has been co-created within it, *it is now incumbent upon you to know your Light.*

You may say to us, "I have heard I carry this Light, others tell me that I carry this Light, but I do not always know that for myself." Is this truth, beloved children? How can you know your Light? *Sit and be still, open your heart, listen!* Your Light comes to you not through your conscious mind but through the wheel of Light at your heart. If you allow yourself to open to this Light you will hear, know, see and understand all that is useful as a basis for your choices as co-creator of your universe. You will walk through this time not as warriors but as beings of peace, harmony, and balance. You will choose to radiate Light in all directions for the sake of all and everything in your universe. It is a very concentric activity.

We do not ask you to stand and march, we ask you to consider that it is more useful *to sit and be still.* In so doing, we ask you to affirm that you are allowing this Light to fill your heart, fill your being, and bring you to a consciousness that connects you to your Light -- which is infinite, compassionate, wise and omniscient. This Light can then guide you from the center of your universe and bring you to a place of balance, peace and harmony for all and everything within your universe. Beloved children, *you can stand in the midst of war and radiate this Light* if you allow it.

: ♦ ♦ :

Will this lead to the transformation of your human plane? Yes. Will this lead to the transformation of your universe? Yes. Is that why you have chosen to be alive at this time? Yes.

Many of you have children or grandchildren, many of you have loved ones, homes, friends, families, and many wonderful things for which you are very grateful. And you may ask, "What of these beings, how are they while I sit and am still? Will they be suffering while I am radiating my Light?" We ask you to sit and be still in this moment, open your heart, allow the Light of Source to fill your heart and listen. You will know the answer. What does your heart tell you? When you choose to carry Light you know in your heart that you are cared for. You allow the Light to carry you through this time and you trust the power of the Light to radiate into your human plane.

We are most grateful that Leia has given us the opportunity to speak with you. Today, we speak to you through human consciousness. At other times [without a conscious channel] if you are still, you can hear your own Totality speak to you as well as the beings of Light who wish to be of service to each and everyone of you -- as they have been to this time and this day, but perhaps without your conscious realization. Understand, children, that this is a plane of freewill choice. This means, although we are with you at all times, *we cannot come to you unless you invoke us*, unless you ask for our help. Then, indeed, we will be most grateful to be of service to you at any time and in any place -- but first you must ask.

Many of you may say, "Masters, why have you not stopped the suffering? Why have you not helped us to do this better, to be better, to be happier, to be healthier, to have lives of peace, harmony and balance? And where is God? Why has God not helped us and delivered us from suffering?" You live on a plane of freewill choice. That which we call Infinite Source -- and which you may call another name, of course -- loves all and everything unconditionally. If you do not invoke its help, if you do not open your heart and being to this

: ♦ ♦ :

Light it cannot help you. It can only come to you and be of service when you request it.

The time of prayer and meditation [referring to the "great experiment" by James Twyman and his group] eased the suffering on your human plane on that day. Can you do this in every day and in every moment? Can you be in "walking meditation"? Can you move with the Light in all things, and at all times, and in all space? In so doing you transform your human plane. Your simple invocations, your simple prayers, your desire to be open and willing, will in and of itself transform your planet. This, we tell you, is a great truth. Do you understand?

Again, we are most grateful for this opportunity to be with you in conscious communication. *Go within, listen to your Light, ask for help and guidance.* Many in this gathering have developed these skills to some level. Certainly, you may help each other to do this if you choose. Understand, we do not judge you -- we cannot -- we can only love you. Understand, if one day it is easier for you than another, the love from Source does not stop coming to your being. You may stop yourself from receiving it -- because you do believe you are not deserving or have not done things well enough -- this does not stop the Light from coming to you! Only you stop it.

Be kind, gentle and compassionate with yourselves as you move through this process of transformation. You may find some places where you have blocked the Light from being within you. Be compassionate and kind to yourselves as you heal what may have stopped the Light from flowing through you. Opening to your path of transformation is a process -- one step at a time. Again we ask you, begin by sitting and being still.

Thank you, beloved children, for this time today. We ask you to know how you are loved.

:♦ ♦:   :♦ ♦:   :♦ ♦:

:♦ ♦:

Ascended Masters Newsletter # 2

Are Your Hearts Open, Beloved Children?

Each of you possesses many wheels of Light in your being. These wheels of Light attach your physical being to the Light that informs you, that fills your body, soul, and spirit with the great gift of Light. Central to your being is the wheel of Light at your heart. At this time of great change for your human plane it is most crucial to allow the opening of your being to the Light that is flowing ever more rapidly into your human form. All of you but the small child here [referring to an infant in the audience] entered this Earth plane at a time of comparative darkness for humanity. Now you have arrived at a time when Light is pouring in to transmute and transform the darkness on your human plane. In this process all of creation is being challenged by this Light, which is asking all beings: *Are your hearts open?* Are the central portals of your beings open to receive the gift of this powerful new energy that is now filling each and every part of your Earth plane?

All of you are being asked if you are willing to carry this light within your human forms as powerfully as it is being offered to you. Are your hearts open to receive this Light? You may respond, "Master, why is it important that my heart be open?" The heart is the most central connecting point within your human being, essential to carry this Light throughout your whole form -- and then to radiate it into the human plane.

All of you [in the audience] have chosen to be conduits of Light -- to receive the Light into your forms primarily through your hearts and then to radiate this Light from your hearts to your

: ◆ ◆ :

planet. This can occur in a never-ending stream. If you open your hearts to receive, and then transmit and radiate, doing such will never exhaust you, for the supply is inexhaustible. The supply of this wondrous, wonderful Light is inexhaustible.

What we have found, however, is that human beings become overwhelmed at the prospect, at the idea of carrying this great Light. The human mind -- or what has been called the ego mind -- can confuse you. Radiating the Light is a mindless act. All that is required is that you agree to be open to carry this Light. We ask you to seriously consider allowing this Light to guide you, instead of your human mind.

Your human mind may decide that you are not worthy of the Light, that you do not know how to carry the Light, that the Light will overwhelm you, that the Light will frighten you. You may decide that the conditions aren't right to carry this Light, for one reason or another, that you are having a bad day and on a bad day you cannot carry this Light as well as on a good day, and so on. To your human mind these things may all be true. But the Light does not have such thoughts.

The Light that emanates from Infinite Source -- you may call this source whatever resonates with you but for the sake of this discourse we shall call it Infinite Source -- is *infinite, compassionate, loving, nurturing, beneficent, benevolent and it is with you NOW*. It is in your physical forms as we speak and it does not ask you to judge whether the conditions are right for it to be in you, it *is* in you. All we ask you to know is that it is there. All we ask you to do is to consider opening your hearts so that you can know this for yourselves.

: ◆ ◆ :

Many of you may say, "Master, I do not know very well how to do this. Perhaps, opening my heart requires something that I have not yet understood. Is there a certain meditation, are there certain words, are there certain invocations, are there certain ways of speaking, or acting, or thinking that can help me do this better? For I do wish to do this better than I do it now."

There is an expression on your human plane: "There is always room for improvement." We will tell you something curious, beloved children. In regard to this Light that you carry *it is already perfectly within you.* In this particular instance there is no room for improvement. You see, you already *do* what you feel you don't do well enough or that you should do better. We ask you to consider that this is so.

Would you be willing to sit with the Light at this moment? We would ask you as your hearts open within you and as you are sitting here in this wonderful radiance if you could simply affirm: *I am carrying this Light.* I am carrying this Light. I am carrying this Light in this moment, and in the next moment, and in the next moment, and in the next moment – and prior to this moment I was also carrying this Light and prior to that moment as well. Now I choose to *consciously know this* -- for my own sake. I AM. I am carrying this Light. From this moment forward, beloved children, you can affirm that you are consciously aware of this.

At this time of awakening for your human plane each day there is more Light than there was the day before -- Light to know and heal and revel in, and to joyously embrace. This Light only continuous to grow in power, infusing all and everything. Every minute parcel of this creation is being inundated with this powerful frequency.

: ♦ ♦ :

Your planet that has slumbered lo these many years is awakening. You have chosen to be alive at a most wondrous time for your human plane, a most glorious time for your planet. You have chosen to be alive and to awake with your planet, to know the power of your Light, to understand that you have agreed to allow your beings to expand while you are alive to carry evermore of this wondrous Light. *It is incumbent upon you to know this* since you have chosen human form at this time.

What does it mean to carry this Light? It means that you will allow this omniscient, all-knowing Light to fill your heart with compassionate grace and wisdom of consciousness. It also means that you may now choose to heal your heart of lifetimes of fear and sadness, of pain, sorrow and suffering. You can heal all this now -- and in its place your heart can fill you with compassion for yourself, first and foremost, and then for all with whom you are connected.

The wisdom of this Light can guide you in ways that your human mind may not understand -- but can learn to accept. It can teach you to *love yourself unconditionally as you are in this moment.* Learn to love yourself first and foremost; this is a most compassionate and wise act, if you choose it. Then share this unconditional love with your human plane.

Now you may say, "Master, there are so many things to fear. What you ask us to accept at this time is incongruent with what we observe upon this planet. We are entering a period of strife, of great difficulty, of lack, of suffering." Each day, beloved children, you observe many things with your human minds that would belie what we have just spoken. How can this planet be

: ♦ ♦ :

evermore filled with great Light when you perceive great suffering and, indeed, when more suffering may be imminent? When it appears that evil men are plodding destructive acts? When you have seen the suffering in your own lives and the lives of others...?

What you see, beloved children, is illusory. The only thing that is real is the Light. Indeed, human beings may be harmed and may choose disembodiment -- but even so, as they leave their physical forms, their Light remains intact. Did you now this, children? Were you consciously aware of such? Although your form may fall away, your Light will not change, it will remain. This does not mean that we encourage you to leave your forms, or to cause other human beings to leave their forms. Instead, we ask you to consider allowing this Light to take care of you while your planet is in the process of rebirthing itself -- transmuting and transforming its energies so that in every corner of your creation it will ultimately be unencumbered Light.

The process [of preparing for war] that you are beholding is a process that some human beings are choosing to engage in. You cannot judge this for you do not know all the reasons why. With your human minds you cannot understand why these human beings are choosing what they do -- but you can invoke the Light for them, if you choose.

You can make a habit of continually invoking this Light for your planet. We would ask you to consider such without an agenda -- for you do not know with your human mind how this transformation [of the Earth plane] will occur. All you can know is that it will. By asking this beneficent, benevolent Light to aid your Earth in its process you leave the Light unencumbered to do what it will do to transmute, transform, and

: ♦ ♦ :

heal the planet. When you give the Light directions as to how you believe things must be, then your ego mind has come into play deciding how the Light must do its work. Remember that you cannot know with your human mind what the agenda is, how to best aid your planet in its awakening.

You can rest assured that this indeed is the agenda: *Your planet will transmute, transform and heal itself.* We promise you that this is so. We ask you again to be conduits of Light, to invoke the Light for the awakening of your human plane, and to consciously trust that this Light will care for you and all and everything in a perfect order that you may not understand.

We know this may be contrary to what some of you hold and believe as your truths. Your truth is sacred to you, honor it. However, we ask you to continue to keep your hearts open and to listen to this Light, for it will guide you and carry you and care for you. This we can promise. What is required from you is to sit and be still, and open your hearts to listen. You will know.

You may discount all that we have spoken here, that this is not your truth, that you cannot own this -- and the Light will still love you. If you wish the Light to take care of you, it will indeed do such -- if you open and allow it. The Light will never judge your choices, it is only benevolent and loving. Do you understand?

We ask you in this moment if you would sit and be still, and open your hearts to listen to this radiance that is with you now. *Know that you are cared for, beloved children; know that you are cared for.* You have not been abandoned on this globe as it races through your universe; you have only been loved in every

: ◆ ◆ :

moment. That love is omnipotent, it is omniscient, and it perfectly informs your being. This is truth.

Allow the Light to heal your hearts, children. Allow it to heal your suffering, allow it to heal your pain. Ask for these things to be transmuted and transformed into healing radiance within your forms. Open to receive this grace. Since you perceive the Earth to be full of suffering invoke the Light to help your planet heal. Ask the Light to help your planet transmute and transform, to help your planet awaken and to help you remain open as a conduit of Light that can create these invocations for your human plane. Can you do this, beloved children? That is all that is asked of you at this time.

We are most grateful, beloved children, for this opportunity to be of service to you. Understand, we do not choose to be worshipped or adored; we are here in service to you. You have called us to you to aid you at this time. We are most grateful for this opportunity of conscious communication and together with all the benevolent beings we share with each and every one the greatest Love and Light of Source. Thank you.

: ♦ ♦ :　　: ♦ ♦ :　　: ♦ ♦ :

: ♦ ♦ :

Ascended Masters Newsletter # 3

In the Light of War

We welcome you, beloved children, to this opportunity for conscious communication with the beings of Light, some of whom you call the Ascended Masters. Of course, what you choose to call us matters little. What is crucial at this time upon your Earth is that you do indeed invoke the Light, request the Light to come to your planet in any way you choose. But understand, children, that even if you did not choose such, we would not judge you. If you would say, Master, to this moment I have not known how to invoke the Light, or that I should have invoked the Light, or that there is a request that I ask for the Light of Source to come to this Earth -- we would not judge you! You see, we are of a realm of beings who are compassionate, who understand quite fully the precepts of unconditional Love and express that to you.

The Light that informs all is unconditionally loving. It does not judge, it does not punish, it does not think, it simply is nurturing. The Light is the Creator Source of all and everything. So, do not be frightened, children, that you have done something wrong or neglected to do anything at all. This Light that fills your body and gives you life has only one function and that is to love you unconditionally as it flows through your being. It is the same with the beautiful trees and all of Creation that exists, the vegetation, the animal population and all that lives in your seas. Everything that you behold on your beautiful planet is filled with the same Light, the same life force, and it is

: ♦ ♦ :

only there with one function: to nourish and love you unconditionally.

You live at a time on your planet when many would choose to ignore or disallow the existence of this very force. (We call it "Infinite Source" in order to keep it open to whatever name you wish to call it, be it God, or Allah, or Brahma, or the energy of the Buddha nature. This matters little, it is your freewill choice to call it what you will. For the sake of this discourse, however, we shall call it "Infinite Source.") So this energy, this Light, this loving force of energy called Infinite Source informs your being, giving you life, animation, and nurturing energy if you allow it to flow through your physical being. All that is asked of you is that you allow it.

As you allow it you consciously invoke its very presence into your human plane -- simply by acknowledging this wonderful, blessed, benevolent Light. You acknowledge it and invoke it simultaneously. You may say, "Ah, here it is, it is filling my form, it is giving me life, it is nurturing me in every way, it is loving me." This is an invocation, beloved children, and it is powerful, indeed.

If you can walk through your day mindful of the fact that you are filled with the Light and love of Source, you then automatically radiate this wondrous, powerful energy into your human plane, blessing all with whom you come in contact. It is the simplest of invocations and very powerful, indeed. If you can consciously acknowledge that this is who you are, you give the gift of this Light to your human plane and to all of Earth.

That is why you have chosen to be alive at this time, to carry this Light consciously within your forms. You live at a very

: ♦ ♦ :

crucial time for Mother Earth, for this wondrous creation that you may call "Ma," which nurtures you in every way. You feed from the breast of this beautiful creation. All that you see in physical form comes from Ma, from Mother Earth.

This beautiful planet upon whose back you ride is awakening now from a deep slumber that she has been in lo these many centuries. She wishes now to consciously activate the Light within her, and you have chosen to ride on her back as she does this. You have *chosen* this, to be alive as a part of Mother Earth during her awakening process. Your physical form consists solely of Mother Earth shaped into a human being. You have chosen to carry and express the powerful, beautiful energy of this creation while you are conscious of carrying the Light of Source in your physical being.

In previous centuries, human beings carried this Light but they were not as consciously aware of it -- nor did they have the capability of being as consciously aware of it as you do now. This is so because your planet, and you with it, is entering an ever-expanding and powerful force field of Light as you float through your universe. In this force field of Light it is now possible to consciously carry this Light in your body more easily. This then gives you great power. Human beings carry more power now than ever before. The electromagnetic force field and the frequency of it are increasing in every moment. You do not even grasp with your conscious minds how powerful this energy is that you are carrying. That is why we come to you at this time, to tell you of the power of the Light that you are carrying now.

If you choose to be sad, the power of this light will make you sadder than ever before. If you choose to be happy, the power of

: ♦ ♦ :

this Light will make you happier than ever before. If you choose to be angry, the power of this Light will make you angrier than ever before, and if you choose to go to war, the war you create will be more devastating than ever before.

How you choose to use this power is your freewill choice. We will never judge you for your choices -- we never have. We will only love you unconditionally, and so does the Light that flows through you in this very moment. However you choose to be, your Light will love you. That is all it can do.

You may say, "Master, what of these evil forces creating this war [in Iraq]? Does this Light still love these beings unconditionally?" Yes, it does. If it loves you in every moment, how can it do other than love all and everything in creation? You may say, "Master, I don't like these beings and this war they've created, I do not like them at all!" And we will say, we still love you if that is your choice. Keep in mind, however, that the energy you carry is more powerful then ever before; it will be even more powerful tomorrow than it is today. If you choose to hate the beings who create this war, this hatred will harm you more than it will the object of your hatred. By choosing to hate or be angry with anyone or anything you would have blocked the Light from its unencumbered path through your body.

If you choose to hate there will still be the power of the energy within you, albeit distorted, powerfully hating or being angry with something or someone. Consequently, the flow of this unconditionally loving Light will be encumbered within your being. The power of it will still be there but you will no longer allow it to be loving. Instead, you will have chosen to turn the power of it to hate or anger.

: ♦ ♦ :

We cannot stop you from doing such if you choose it. We can only come to you when you request our help. Then we are offering you instantly unconditional love. We will also suggest to you to sit, be still, listen, and to ask to transmute and transform this energy of hatred and anger. You cannot get rid of it, but you can change the nature of it. (You cannot get rid of anything, all is and always will be.) You can, however, transmute it and transform it back to the loving energy that can then once again flow unencumbered throughout your form.

We urge you to sit, be still, request help, and invoke the beings of Light -- or the Light itself --and say, "Help me transmute and transform the energy that is blocking the Light from flowing through me unencumbered." If you do this, the Light will help you. The Light will *always* come to you and aid you in healing whatever has become disharmonic within you.

You may then ask, "Will this stop the war? If I simply learn to love unconditionally, will this stop the war?" We ask you, children, is it your function to stop war or is it your function to unconditionally carry this Light as fully as you can?

There is a way to answer that question for yourselves. If you would sit quietly at this moment you can become aware that you have a spinning wheel of Light in your heart. Within that wheel of Light is a direct connection to your Higher Self, your connection to your Light. All of you in this gathering are receiving help in this moment, if you choose to accept it, to feel this wheel of Light in your heart, to go within to the very center of it and listen to your Light. It will tell you directly what your function is, what you are asked to concentrate on at this time. If you simply sit still and listen you will hear and know the truth for yourself.

: ◆ ◆ :

You may say, "Master, what of this war, how does it relate to me, how does it affect me, and what can I do?" Children, when sadness comes to you for what you are observing, allow yourselves to weep. When pain comes to you because of what you are observing, feel the pain. When fear comes to you because of what you are seeing on your human plane, allow the fear -- and then request the Light to heal you and trust that you will be healed.

There are frightening and terrible things occurring on your human plane at this time and you are human, you are part of OM, ONE. You cannot avoid this and you are not asked to do so. Instead, you are asked to remember your primary purpose.

You may choose to be angry or you may choose to hate the human beings who are making these choices because you do not wish to feel these feelings. You are here to feel these things! Allow them to process through your human beings, allow yourself to transmute and transform these energies, allow yourselves to invoke the help of the beings of Light and heal your beings.

As you do this, you transform your planet, you heal Ma and help her awaken, you allow the Light to flow through you more unencumbered than ever before, and you bring about the dawning of a new time for the human plane where peace will reign.

Each of you has a war to fight. It is within yourselves, in all the places that you carry traces from this and many lifetimes when you have suffered. It is time to finally heal these things -- for all time. You can do that now. You can heal yourselves more easily

: ♦ ♦ :

than ever before with the power of this Light that you now carry.

Armageddon is within. Face your battles, face your fears, face your pain, face your sorrow. Ask the Light to help you transmute and transform it. Become whole and complete, and consciously carry your Light for the sake of all and everything. That is why you are here.

Do you understand? Your planet is entering dark days. The suffering will not diminish in the near future. But you can hold the Light! Even in the darkest hour you can be Light!

We know some of you are afraid of this task. We ask you to heal those fears, transmute and transform them. We ask you to go within and listen to your hearts where your Light anchors to your physical beings, and you will hear something very important. What you will hear is: You are cared for in every moment. This Light never abandons you, never! You may choose to walk away from it -- it will *never* leave you. Even when you loose your physical form, it is with you, it *is* you, it cannot separate from you. Try as you might to rid yourself of your Light, it is impossible. We ask you to consciously know this to be so.

That is our most fervent request at this time. Know you are Light! Know this Light is unconditionally loving. Know this Light fills your being; there is no place in your body that is not Light. Know that you can carry it consciously. Know that it is more powerful than ever before.

And know that if you do not choose to carry this Light consciously, it does not abandon you nor does it leave you. You

: ♦ ♦ :

can invoke it at any moment and it will always be unconditionally loving and will aid you in carrying it more strongly than ever before.

If you choose to consciously allow this, know that you are cared for by this Light in every moment as you walk on this human plane. Even when you choose to leave this human plane you are still cared for by this Light. That is what you are asked to understand this day.

We thank you, beloved children, once again for this opportunity to speak with you in conscious communication. Understand children, that each of you is receiving information directly. We may speak here through another but if you listen within you will hear this for yourselves. Know how you are loved!

:♦ ♦:   :♦ ♦:   :♦ ♦:

Ascended Masters Newsletter # 4

Now is the Time to Heal Your History

Did you know, beloved children, that each and every one of you is connected to what we call your "Totality," your connection to the Light of Source? Instead of the term "Source," you may wish to call it God, Allah, the Buddhic ray, Brahma, or any one of a number of names that would aid you in understanding Infinite Source, that is your choice.

:♦ ♦:

Today, we wish to talk about the concept of "Totality." Although you may use this term interchangeably, if you wish, with "Higher Self," we have found that your human minds have a limited concept of Higher Self. When you hear the term Totality, however, your minds are able to embrace a larger concept. This concept, if you will, describes the essence of your being. You are human at this time and in this space -- but you are much more than you can witness with your human mind. You carry within you a map of the history of your being from time immemorial; it reaches from before all time until, indeed, after time as you know it upon your Earth plane. Your history -- past, present, and future -- is transcribed in the essence of your Totality.

Does the energy of your Totality connect you to Infinite Source? It *is* the energy of Infinite Source. It is all and everything that you have ever been or ever will be. This energy is constantly evolving. It is not at all static in nature. As we have mentioned previously, nothing about who you are in any given moment is as it has been nor as it shall be. And yet, existing in every moment is everything you have ever been or ever will be -- but from moment to moment this is evolving!

If you arose yesterday in your Earth time and you said, I am unhappy and these are the reasons why, you can give yourself permission to awaken tomorrow and decide that all the reasons for your past unhappiness are no longer valid. And that would be true. You can say at any time, I choose to be happy and these are the reasons why I have chosen happiness in my life. The reasons why you were unhappy before were valid for *that* time, they were your truth *then*.

: ♦ ♦ :

If you changed your mind, however, you did not make a mistake, you did nothing wrong. Indeed, from our perspective you never make a mistake. We do not watch, judge, and evaluate your movement from day to day and moment to moment. We have found, however, that human beings do choose to do such. Not only do they do this for themselves but they do that for the other human beings in their environment as well!

You may say to someone, yesterday you made a mistake and today I remember it and I am still angry because of the mistake you made yesterday. You may believe it is valid and authentic to speak your truth about something that occurred in the past and how you are still feeling about it. In doing so you disallow the opportunity for change that is always available to you. In every moment you are given the permission to evolve -- and to be valid in a completely different way than you were the moment before.

If you do evolve, others may come to you and say, "I do not understand you, you are confusing me, yesterday you were angry and today you are not and yet I do the same thing today that I did yesterday, why is it that you are no longer angry with me?" You could answer, "I have chosen to evolve to a new place of being. What disturbed me previously no longer disturbs me, I freed myself of the discomfort that I had imposed upon myself and I understand that I can choose a new way of being."

Beloved children, this is what is occurring on your Earth plane now: Your ability to change and evolve is more powerfully available to you today than it was yesterday, and will be even more so tomorrow. This beautiful planet upon which you reside is continuously exposing itself -- as it is moving through time

: ♦ ♦ :

and space -- to vibrational energies that are very powerful. The evolution of every being's Totality is accelerating more rapidly now than ever before. What you have clung to as your history is slowly dissolving energetically.

If you choose to continue to cling to your history you will only find this increasingly uncomfortable because you are evolving away from your history. For instance, if you say, as a child my life was very painful and I still remember this pain, and because of it I am as I am now, we will tell you, yes, that was your truth then. Now you live in a time when you can allow these painful energies to dissolve, transmute, transform, and heal. You can choose a new way of being; you may say, yes indeed, I do have this history -- but my heart is healing, my being is healing, I am more at peace than ever before.

What we have found, however, is if we aid human beings in recognizing that they can heal themselves this becomes very frightening to them. The next thought they will have is, if I can no longer carry this history as I have known it, and identify with it as who I am in this lifetime, I am frightened because I do not know who I am.

Most human beings cannot let go of their histories. However, to be alive today it is necessary to allow your histories to heal. Only then can you move evermore rapidly into who you are becoming as you are evolving, which is a human being closely aligned with his or her Totality. As your Totality is evolving, the Light that is flooding through all time and space is flowing through your history from who you have been in other lifetimes to who you are now and beyond to who you will be in the future. As your totality is evolving into the Light it is asking you to let go, become whole and complete, and to allow

: ♦ ♦ :

yourselves to heal and move with your planet. It is asking you to move with the Earth plane into resolution, clearing, and healing. Now is the time for this to be done.

You may say, "Master, what of all the human beings who are choosing to cling to their history, respond to it, and even be at war because of it?" We will say to you, children, yes, that will be the choice for those who insist upon clinging to their histories. If you do not let go of your histories you will be at war within yourselves -- and that may escalate to your choosing to be at war with those around you. You will be angry because you are uncomfortable and wish to blame it on others. But the discomfort you feel within comes from within you! It will never be due to the human beings around you, it is always coming from within.

All of you have suffered great pain, in this lifetime and in past lifetimes. This is the time to heal, transmute, and transform your painful histories. Can you let go, children, can you heal now? If you do this now you will experience a glorious freedom that allows you to be saturated by this Light and live in a universe free of suffering. For that is indeed the gift that is coming to you now if you choose to accept it.

You may say, "Well, Master, I may choose this. But what of the other human beings around me, what if they do not, what if they choose to continue suffering, will I not be lonely? Will I not experience pain in my heart as I watch others continue to suffer? Must I then teach them to be as I will choose to be?" We ask you to understand that your Totality includes your universe, all and everything with which you interact at any given time. If you choose to accept the Light flooding through you now, and do so without expectation simply because you wish freedom

: ♦ ♦ :

from suffering for yourself, your whole universe will shift and move with you! We do not tell you how, we cannot tell you how, for each of you is a unique being of Light; you must allow this to occur for you in its own unique manner. Do this without expectation, trust, and know that your universe will move with you. That is all we can say in this regard.

We understand you wish to know more as to how that can be so. Inherent in what we speak of is the crucial element of trust. If I let go of my pain, sorrow, suffering, anger, blame, guilt, and shame, if I let go of such and ask this bounteous, beautiful Light to help me heal -- can I trust that my universe will change and I will live in harmony, balance and healing? We can say unequivocally, yes, this is truth, this is so. Indeed. Absolutely. It is so.

You must wish this for yourself with every fiber of your being because as you allow yourself to heal, as your history bubbles up within you, you will pass through moments of pain. Most human beings stop this process not because they have felt the pain, but because they are afraid to feel the pain. And yet their fear of pain ultimately leads to more pain, unhappiness, and suffering. Children, understand that *your fear of the pain you may experience as you review your history is a greater discomfort than any pain you will ever feel.* If you allow yourselves to feel the pain and allow the light to heal and transform it you will gain the freedom you seek to be in peace, harmony, balance, and yes, JOY as you walk this plane.

For most human beings acknowledging their pain, their guilt, their shame requires an act of great courage. Yet, your Totalities are evolving, you are moving into the Light, whether you agree to this or not in your conscious mind. You chose to be alive

: ♦ ♦ :

now and with that you agreed to allow this Light to flood your beings.

However, if you choose to continue to suffer the cost to your beings will only increase and life will become more and more uncomfortable. Many of you are already choosing to transition and simply leave the Earth plane; for one reason or another it is too painful to stay. Many of you are still choosing to blame others for your suffering. As a result, they have become angry and more warlike and they, beloved friends, will also choose to leave the Earth plane in time. We would never judge their choices. We only have compassion and love for all of you. We encourage you in any way we can to let go and allow the Light to heal your history so that you can accept this powerful Light more fully within your beings and claim your birthright as beings of Light. Powerful, powerful beings of Light! Do you understand?

In response to a question regarding the fear of possible terrorism the Masters said among other things: You believe that in this time on your planet there are more reasons to be frightened; you believe this, it is just a belief. At any given time upon the Earth there have always been things that can frighten you, it simply appears that there are more things now to frighten you than ever before. As a mass of consciousness your planet has agreed to believe that terrible things must happen now. If you believe this, than you invite such into your universe and you will co-create that terrible things will happen. Then you can be correct about your assumptions. We ask you to understand that as you heal yourselves and allow the Light to flow unencumbered through your being, part of the agreement that you make is that you are carried by your Light in every

: ♦ ♦ :

moment. And then there is nothing to fear -- unless you choose to fear and then, of course, it would be useful to be afraid.

Thank you, beloved children, once again for this opportunity for conscious communication. As always, we offer you unconditional love and Light from Source. Know how you are loved.

:♦ ♦:   :♦ ♦:   :♦ ♦:

Ascended Masters Newsletter # 5

A Message from the Christos

At the onset Linda shares that she has a clear sense that today's message is coming from the Christ consciousness, or "Christos" as we call it, and she comments that this is a first for a group channeling of this format.

Isn't it interesting, beloved children, that this one called Leia has agreed to channel in conscious communication that which you have called the Christ consciousness. For you see, she chose to come in as a Jewish child at her birth; and so we remind her that the one commonly called Christ chose the same for his embodiment. He also came in as a Jewish child. Of course, you are all aware of that.

:♦ ♦:

What we would wish you to understand is the *universality* of that which you call the Christ consciousness. In addition, we would wish you to understand what thoughts, what ideas have become attached to this concept of Christ as well as the concepts of Allah, of Brahma, of Buddha, and of God.

Each of you here sitting in this time and space hears these terms -- and instantly images or ideas arise in your mind. You hear the term "God," or "Allah," or "Buddha," or "Christ" -- and each of you will have your own *unique* response to those words.

We ask you, children, to respond honestly and to accept however you respond -- there are no wrong answers, there are no right answers. We ask each of you to honor the perfection of your being in this moment as you respond to these names. You have not gotten it wrong; you have not gotten it right; it is perfect for you. Can you honor the perfection of who you are, each being in this room, in this moment, as you are, with whatever thoughts arise in your mind? Those words are charged with incredible emotion based on your history and many lifetimes -- lifetimes in which you have been Hindu, Buddhist, Christian, Jewish, Muslim. You have all been such. Did you know that, children?

And yet, in the perfection of this moment as you hear these names your heart will respond differently to each of those terms. However, you have all been such, and more: Male, female, mother, father, sister, brother, robber, victim, murderer... You have taken your own lives, you have suffered terribly, and at times you have been the perpetrator of suffering. Yet in this lifetime when you hear a story, a name, a term, you find yourself evaluating and judging, do you not? Would it be true to say that this is so?

: ♦ ♦ :

Whether you know it or not, you have great feeling and emotion charging through you [when you hear such] based on your karmic history. Simply put, your karmic history is the pain that you have felt, the joy that you have felt, the emotion that you have felt as events have unfolded in your many lifetimes. That is what charges the response to what you hear at any moment.

You may say, I have never liked Jewish people -- and you may not even know why. Or you may say, my father did not like Jewish people, so I have then chosen to like Jewish people -- but I have found few that I could really like [chuckle], and so forth and so on; it is true.

There is a prevalent dynamic in your land and in your world where many people dislike those who dress differently, have different habits, perhaps different facial hair, and thus appear nefarious because some people who share these attributes have caused great harm. On that basis it becomes easy to decide not to like any of the people who have similar attributes. Furthermore, it becomes easy to blame those people as a whole for the behavior of some in their midst. Such tendencies are prevalent in the minds of human beings at this time.

Beloved children, what we ask you to consider -- for your own sakes -- is that *with your human minds you cannot know or understand what is occurring on your planet at this time.* You may have opinions about what you are beholding, it may cause your heart great pain, you may feel fear, or you may have suffered directly as a result of some of the things that are occurring on the human plane. And yet, if you choose to evaluate or judge any of this you will do so from ignorance.

: ♦ ♦ :

We are not saying that you aren't smart or intelligent people. We are simply saying that *you do not know, cannot know with your human minds why things are unfolding as they are.* You cannot understand the complete picture because the human mind is very literal, you see. It is good at assessing the three dimension of your Earth plane but not much more than that.

We would ask you to consider this when you are evaluating what is disturbing you -- and it is disturbing you, all of you. This you may wish to acknowledge. Understand that *everything you are observing on your planet at this time is designed for the human mind to think in terms of separation and fear -- and that this is an illusion.*

Children, if you allow yourselves to think in terms of separation and fear you will judge. When you choose such a path, however, you find in each and every instant that it is painful -- and that it perpetuates the suffering on your planet at this time.

Why are you here? Why have you chosen to be alive? Why have you chosen to allow yourselves to be privy to this message that we offer you this day -- and that we offer you continuously? *You have chosen to be alive to dispel the illusion of separation and to touch a knowing of oneness in the core of your being.*

Your being is more than your physical form. As you sit in this time and space you feel encased in your bodies and yet, in truth, you are more than you behold, much more. Each and every being is the Light of Infinite Source. ("Infinite Source" is not a term that we have used to this point. It encompasses all the other names that we have used here today such as Buddha, Allah, Brahma, God; they are just the different faces, if you

:♦ ♦:

will, that human beings have given the concept that we shall call "Infinite Source.") This is *the Light that informs your body, beloved children, it is infinite, it is omniscient, it is all-knowing* and while your human mind is limited in understanding the true nature of reality, this Light of Infinite Source has no difficulty understanding that there is no separation, that separation is an illusion!

You can access this Light of Infinite Source and allow it to connect to your conscious mind to guide you to this knowing, to this realization. Did you know that? You are most fortunate indeed, beloved children, for you live in a time when this is more easily possible for *homo sapiens* than in any other time that *homo sapiens* has existed on your plane. You live at a time when this becomes more easily obtained, this understanding, this connecting of your conscious mind to your Light than ever before. It is a wondrous time to be alive, wondrous indeed. Beloved children, we would encourage you to consider this conscious connection to your Light!

Your heart is the seat of this Light and as you call it into your heart it flows consciously through the very core of your human being. Then you can say to your mind, "Relax please, I wish to listen to my Light to know my truth." *In that stillness, that quiet that precedes enlightenment, you can know there is no separation, you are all one, you are all OM.*

When you let go of judgment, when you let go of fear, when you let go of what the various names of Infinite Source have meant to you, your heart opens. Compassion and wisdom become the cornerstone of your existence, and life becomes a vehicle of healing and transformation -- not only for yourself but for your whole universe. Do you understand?

: ♦ ♦ :

Beloved children, we ask you for your own sakes to seriously consider what we offer to you today. Your light is formidable. Day by day it grows stronger within your human forms. Awaken to it, allow it to fill you, understand the perfection of your beings. You are not separate, you are one, you are whole, you are complete as an embodiment of all that is. In every lifetime you have had you have touched all there is. This knowledge resides within you.

When you choose to see only one side, you do not see the whole picture. How can you hate your brother when he is you and you are he? Do you understand what we speak? *Open your hearts, children, allow this Light to fill you, know the truth of who you are.* It is a simple thing, it is a simple thing.

Love and Light to One and All

:♦♦:   :♦♦:   :♦♦:

:♦♦:

Ascended Masters Newsletter # 6

A Message from St. Germain

Before we started with the channeling Linda had shared an experience we had earlier in the day when we connected with the golden-white Light in a new way. She had told the group that this intensified energy was uncomfortable at first and that she had to surrender to it for the discomfort to abate.

Upon opening to channel, Linda indicated that the Ascended Master associated with the violet flame, St. Germain, would be speaking to us today. He suggested that we invoke healing and blessings for Mother Earth and all who reside upon her -- which we did.

Prior to this conscious communication Leia has spoken with you of an experience that she and Manalus chose of allowing the Light of Source to flow into their human forms in a very structured manner and then as it flowed through them to allow this Light to flow into Mother Earth. This experience came to Leia and Manalus at their request. As your beloved friend here [the host of this event] has spoken, we cannot come unbidden to you, for this is a plane of freewill choice. We are here only in service to you.

So, Leia and Manalus made the request, once again, to open more fully to a conscious connection, to yoke their minds to their Light, if you will. What is this Light we speak of? It is the Light of Infinite Source. Whatever name you wish to call it -- it

: ◆ ◆ :

could be God, Allah, Brahma -- it is all-knowing, omniscient, compassionate, loving, nurturing, healing, transformational, benevolent, beneficent energy -- the *Light of Source.*

What they have chosen is to allow this Light to connect directly and consciously to their human minds. To listen to this Light as it anchors into their hearts, for this is the most central point of entry for this beneficent Light. They have chosen to listen consciously to that still, small voice within and allow it to guide them in their every movement while they walk Mother Earth in human form.

Beloved children, you have *all* agreed to the same. Prior to your birth you agreed to be these vehicles of Light -- in human form. But as Leia has mentioned this planet appears to be less and less comfortable. In recent days you have had many events -- and you will have many more -- that have appeared to your conscious mind to be very disturbing. So it is less likely that you would enjoy being in your physical bodies in a conscious manner.

Indeed, Leia has found that because she has the gift of communication with the Light (as do you all) she often chooses to withdraw from her form. The expression you might use is "being out of body." Lately, she has been out of body as much as possible without consciously being aware of it. The term she uses is "being on auto pilot"-- rather than to be fully engaged within her human form, anchoring the Light into her body as she walks upon Mother Earth.

And yet, her physical form has been uncomfortable because of this. In addition, she is not fulfilling the agreements she made prior to birth to utilize all of her gifts and skills that she chose in

: ♦ ♦ :

this embodiment. She had agreed to allow all of them to come forth from her being and to share them with Mother Earth. Some of you might find this to be true for your own personal situation as well.

Understand children, you have chosen to be alive now to carry this Light fully in your forms, anchoring it into Mother Earth, sharing and radiating it throughout your planet. You have agreed to use all of your capabilities while you are fully alive and fully conscious in your human forms. It is crucial children, that you know this for your own sakes!

Your planet is changing now very rapidly. Mother Earth has been slumbering for lo these many centuries and she is awakening now. You have chosen to help her with that process -- for you are extensions of Mother Earth. Understand, your bodies come from Mother Earth. Each piece of food that you place between your lips comes from Ma. It has shaped your forms. You are not separate from her. You *are* Mother Earth.

Your planet carries Light. You carry Light. By being conscious conduits of Light, this Light flows through you and into your planet and becomes part of the transformation process that will awaken Mother Earth from her slumber.

Children, open your hearts and share your love and your Light with the beautiful creatures -- those who swim in your waters and those who walk on your Earth. Nurture all that rises from the soil on your planet. Know that beings of Light are connected to each and every drop of water, every snowflake, and every grain of sand. All of your planet is Light!

: ◆ ◆ :

Is it much of a leap then to realize that you, each and every atom of your being, is also Light? But to use an expression, "therein lies the rub." Is it not easier for you children, to look at this creature [our dog who was present in the gathering] and believe that this beautiful animal is filled with Light -- than it is for you to look in the mirror each day and say "*I am also carrying this Light*"? Is this not truth, children?

That is why we have agreed to be with you this day. To bring you this joyful news.

You may say, "Master, do you understand that even if we carry the Light as fully in our bodies as we can, there are still things that are uncomfortable as we are walking on this planet? There are moments of great pain and sorrow, of fear, of worry, that also accompany our journey on this planet." Yes, children, we know all these things. You have lived many, many lifetimes -- as have we. We have all had human forms prior to opening to our Light.

We know of your pain, we know of your confusion, we know of your anger, we know of your sense of recrimination. How badly you feel regarding your own selves for the things you have done wrong, for the mistakes you have made and the times you have wished you were not angry. How badly you feel for the things you said or did in those moments. We know of those times. And we know that the greatest punishment that you can give yourselves is to say, "I do not deserve my Light" and thus to close yourselves to your Light.

You see, this Light has never left you. It cannot. It is who you are. But you, you can -- and have on more than one occasion -- closed your heart to your Light. Children, there is no greater

: ♦ ♦ :

pain that you will ever experience on this human plane than closing your heart to your own Light. No one, nothing will ever harm you more than you will harm yourselves in doing this to yourselves!

You may say, that is not true. My child, or my husband, or my parent did or said terrible things to me and it was very painful. Yes, we understand it was painful. But we also ask you to realize that you *chose* your response to that experience.

We ask you to consider the option that if someone says or does something painful, *you can choose to keep your heart open.* You can choose to love yourself with your Light and perhaps even, in response to the experience, radiate a compassionate Light to the one who chose such an action towards you.

You might say, "Well, that person doesn't deserve the Light." We understand that this would be your natural reaction. But we also remind you that closing your heart to your own Light harms you -- whereas radiating your Light does the opposite. Keeping your heart open in response to a hurtful activity by another is a way of nurturing yourself.

Another response would be to close your heart and cause yourself great pain. Do you believe that is what you deserve? Do you believe you deserve to suffer because the other has done this, that, or the other thing? Do you deserve to suffer, children?

We ask you in this moment to open your hearts. See laser beams of Light from Source enter the very epicenter of the wheel of Light, the chakra of Light, at your heart. See a laser beam of violet Light and a laser beam of golden Light entering into the

: ♦ ♦ :

very center of the wheel of Light at your heart. Listen to your Light. Listen to your Light. What is it telling you?

This Light is all knowing; it is omniscient; it is unconditionally loving you with great compassion. All it wishes is to be acknowledged and to be allowed to freely flow through your forms and anchor your beings to Mother Earth so that you can be conduits of this unconditionally loving Light for your planet at this time. That is the greatest gift you can give yourselves. Know this to be true.

You are Light, children. Loving Light. Others may choose disharmonious behavior patterns and you may choose to respond with anger. You may choose to respond with pain. Forgive yourselves. Be compassionate toward yourselves. Then breathe the Light. Heal yourselves first.

In the past we have said something to Leia and Manalus that at first took them aback. We have asked them to consider loving themselves before all others -- loving themselves first with this Light before they can love their world, their universe, and all that inhabits it. Then, and only then, can they radiate this Light. Then, and only then, can they respond to that which is painful by radiating Light.

Loving yourselves first and foremost strengthens your connection to your Light. This then opens you ever further to healing and transformation within.

You may say, "Where will this lead? Are we ascending, will we become beings of Light?" Yes, you will. That is what your planet will do, Mother Earth and all who ride her back and choose to be alive, and to awaken to their Light at this time, will

: ♦ ♦ :

become fully awakened, fully alive, fully transformed and healed.

Leia finds that a tall order. She is not quite sure she is up to it. Understand, beloved children, you do not do this alone. Each of you at any given moment of your day is not only carrying this formidable Light, you are also surrounded by it; indeed, there is a veritable sea of beings of Light surrounding you. Your universe is filled with help. All you need do is ask.

It is not for your human mind to do more than ask for help. Open your beings and say, "I will yoke my mind to my Light and allow it to guide me." It is a simple thing -- but you will test this. And we ask you to be compassionate for when you do test it.

We also tell you once again what we have said many times: You will not be better tomorrow than you were yesterday. *You are already perfect,* right now in this moment. You will not be improving or getting better because you weren't worse before. At every moment you are perfect as you are for that moment. Each moment is a foreordained journey that you have agreed to bring you to this aware awakening. Your path is perfect. It has been perfect all along.

Everything you haven chosen to experience has been for one reason only: To awaken you to your Light. In fact, you can trust that each moment will continue to be perfect for that process to unfold within.

We ask you once again to listen with your own heart, to allow these beams of Light to fill you. Listen clearly for yourselves to know that as you consciously awaken and allow this Light to

: ♦ ♦ :

radiate through you, you never need to fear anything. There will be no reason to fear. This Light cares for you. It takes care of you. We ask you to know this to be truth.

We thank you, beloved children, for this opportunity to be with you once again in conscious communication. We thank you for your invocations and blessings for your wondrous planet. You are powerful beings of Light. When you bless your Earth with your Light it is transforming your universe. Know this to be true. -- So it is done.

:♦ ♦:   :♦ ♦:   :♦ ♦:

Ascended Masters Newsletter # 7

Releasing Your Past – Accepting Your Light
A Message from the Christos

At the beginning of the channeling Linda indicated that she felt the Christos energy coming through. We call the "Christos" the divine Light from Source that has been present since the beginning of creation. In other cultural traditions this Light may be called by other names, such as Brahma or the Buddhic Ray. By choosing the name Christos we are not implying that Christianity is superior to any of the other traditions that concern themselves with the Light from Source.

:♦:

Understand, beloved children, whatever frequency you have chosen to connect with on the human plane at this time -- that you have requested to come through Leia to speak with you -- is an energy that you have always known. It is an energy with which you have always been connected and an energy that has spoken directly to you before. You are connected to that which you may call the Light of the Christos not only in this moment. It is a simply a request that you have made that we come through Leia at this time.

We use the term "we" to describe this energy because it is not singular in nature. It is not separated from anything. It is all and everything. As we speak through Leia, that is the way we can describe ourselves.

If you look at the sky, at the sun, at the moon, at the stars, if you look out upon the land that you have and the beautiful things that grow upon your land, and even as you look within this abode, if you look around this space in which you sit, what are you sitting on? What is beneath your feet? What have you just eaten? All of these things of which we speak carry the Light of this Christos. This beneficent loving Light is in everything in Creation. *All is composed of the energy of the Light of the Christos.*

If you choose to extrapolate from that which we have just said, then you who are sitting in these chairs must also be completely composed of the energy of the Christos. Why would this Light be in the stone on the land but not in you? Indeed, what would stop this energy from being in you? Paradoxically, if you observe your trees and your plants, you can say, Ah Yes! I see this wonderful energy in the trees, in the leaves, and I can call it

: ♦ ♦ :

the Light of the Christos -- but I cannot feel it and know it in myself!

Only one thing can stop you from allowing this energy to flow through you unencumbered. *One thing only.* It is your conscious human mind.

We would ask you, beloved friends, would you consider a simple exercise? Would you consider allowing this Light to be a conscious awareness in this moment? A part of your mind may say, Yes, but... Yes, I would like to do this, but I cannot. There may be an energy that wishes to stop the conscious awareness of this wondrous Light with thoughts such as, "I cannot completely accept that I am the Light of the Christos because I have done terrible things, I have made terrible mistakes, I have caused others to suffer, and I am suffering. I am afraid of what tomorrow will bring. I carry great pain because of yesterday or even today. And because I have carried this pain, I cannot trust myself, I cannot love myself, and I certainly cannot accept this Light of the Christos. Indeed, it may be in the trees, in the birds, in the water and in everything in Creation, but none of those things have ever been human and done all the terrible things that we have all done as human beings." That is what your mind may say.

Indeed, for centuries on your human plane, eons, time beyond time, this has been so. Human beings cannot believe that they are as deserving and, in fact, filled with the same Light as all you see around you. Interesting to note, is it not?

And yet, if you were to ask the Light of the Christos if you deserve this Light, that would not even be a concept that could be entertained by this beneficent energy. You see, *this Light*

: ♦ ♦ :

simply is. It already exists within you and it has never questioned whether you deserve it or not. It is an incomprehensible concept to this Light to wonder whether it should be within you. It cannot wonder; it can only be.

This Light is what you would call, in very limited, human terms, "unconditionally loving Light." This is an interesting term that human beings have great difficulty accepting and understanding. Unconditionally loving Light. It is there within you. It did not evaluate or judge whether it should be within you. That is an impossible concept for this Light to entertain.

This Light is your Higher Self. All, as Jesus said, can do as he has done and assume the mantel of the Christos. All that remains is simply to accept who you are already.

You may say, "I must do something to deserve this. I must climb a certain mountain, behave in a certain way, eat certain foods, say certain prayers, scourge my being in certain ways, pay certain sums of money to some religious organization and attend it regularly..." And all of these things have been useful for human beings to choose to do. None of this can be judged.

But it is not necessary. *All that is necessary is simply to say: I accept my Light.* As Manalus is fond of saying, and so are the beings of Light, *the truth is simple.*

Yes, you have lived thousands of lifetimes and you have all done terrible things as human beings. Not only have you done terrible things, but terrible things have happened to you. You may say, "If I am this Light -- as logically you might have to concede -- why would I have chosen to do terrible things or have allowed terrible things to happen to me?" We answer with

⋮ ◆ ◆ ⋮

another truth that you know. You have chosen to live -- and have been given the grace to live in human form -- on a plane of freewill choice. You then, upon departure from one lifetime and before entering another lifetime, have discussed matters with your own Light, your own Higher Self. At that time you chose the karma that you believe you must perpetrate during your subsequent incarnation.

However, now we have come to an interesting time on your human plane. This is a time that some have called "the end time." For centuries, human beings have made many dire predictions regarding such, have they not?

In truth, beloved children, we will tell you something you may wish to know: *You are living in a wondrous time. It is a perfect time to heal your history.* The veils are thinning between the planes and your Earth is healing itself from its history. Now you are capable of doing the same. It is easier now than ever. *You can say, "I will release my history, I will open and release my karmic history." You can let it go. You can drop it. You can heal your past. You can open and accept your Light. You can.*

Remember that you can ask for help from the beings Light to do these things, if you choose. If you choose. We do not ordain or dictate these things. We cannot. All we can do is love you unconditionally. When invited into your physical being and into your heart (which is the main entry point) with great alacrity we will flood your form with Light. All that is required is that you ask for this.

We ask you, children, to be kind, to be patient and to have compassion for yourselves first and foremost. Love yourselves. Understand historically this is something you are very

: ♦ ♦ :

unaccustomed of doing. But also understand that you can do this now. You can do this now.

The Christos invited questions from the audience.

<u>Question</u>: How might I be aware of the presence of this Light?

<u>Answer</u>: It is a simple thing. In your meditation sit before a beautiful natural creation, such as a tree, and as you open your heart, the wheel of Light, see yourself entering this beautiful natural creation that you call your tree. Feel the radiance of this wondrous creation envelope you and sing to you its soothing song of love and Light. Know the same Light that fills this wondrous creation is singing and harmonizing to the essence of your being. Your Light can blend with this golden radiance. Become one, OM. Know that this is the truth of who you are as well. Your tree trusts that the soil of Mother Earth will nourish it -- just as the soil of Mother Earth nourishes you. It trusts, that the Sun and the rain will nourish it -- just as the Sun and the rain nourish you. And it trusts that it will know its seasons with wisdom and omniscience. It knows when to drop its leaves and when to let new leaves grow. Let the rhythm of the cycles fill you. Allow yourself to be One. Affirm this Light that loves you, takes care of you, and rest in this knowing.

:♦ ♦:   :♦ ♦:   :♦ ♦:

:♦ ♦:

Ascended Masters Newsletter # 8

St. Germain on Abundance (and Marriage)

We welcome you, beloved children, to this opportunity for conscious communication with the beings of Light, but do understand we have been with all of you many, many times, beloved children. As you consciously request our guidance we will continue to be with you, if you allow.

You reside on this beautiful planet called Mother Earth in a most wondrous, beautiful creation. It is a plane of freewill choice where you reside in human form, a most wondrous form that carries great Light within. You live in what is, indeed, a Garden of Eden.

Your beautiful planet provides you with all that you need to live. All your needs are met if you allow it to be so on this most beautiful creation, your Mother Earth. What a wondrous thing to experience, to be alive now on this most beautiful planet, and to know with your conscious minds that everything you perceive is Light. You are Light, your planet is Light, and it all comes from a most beneficent Source.

If you could allow the natural order of things on your most beautiful, beneficent planet, then all of you would know that this planet was designed by this most beneficent Light to give you all you need to live. Air to breathe, sun to warm you, Earth to feed you.

: ◆ ◆ :

And yet, you may wonder -- and you may even ask us -- why aren't my needs being met? This is a good question. Most human beings live in fear of lack; they live in fear and worry that tomorrow their needs will not be met because, in their estimation, yesterday their needs had not been met.

Here you live under these most beautiful conditions, suffering and in need, if truth be known. We do not judge you for such. We have all been human, and we know what can happen when one is in human form. One can forget about this beneficent Light that takes care of all. However, the Light can only take care of you if you allow it.

One can forget about that truth when one is in human form. I myself, when I wore the mantel of the one called Bacon, [St. Germain is referring here to his incarnation as Francis Bacon] I landed in debtors prison more than once, you see. I would forget to pay my debt and those who had supplied things to me did not take kindly to this, so my punishment was to be incarcerated for my forgetfulness.

The beings of Light that you call Ascended Masters have all had human form and we know of the fear of lack and the suffering that can accompany such.

We also, if truth be known, recognize all of you as beings of Light who are with us in your enlightened forms where we are, where there is no time and space. We are connecting to each and every one of you. You, in turn, in your enlightened form as beings of Light are observing that portion of your Totality that is in human form. And we all are saying to your human selves: "We love you unconditionally and we support you as beings of Light."

: ♦ ♦ :

We also wish to offer you our love and support in your awakening to the true nature of your wonderful planet -- and of a concept that can be called *abundance*. It is a concept that we would wish to speak to you about in this gathering.

What does the term "abundance" mean? It is not prosperity or the accumulation of wealth. When you hear the term abundance it may bring a vision to you of a cornucopia filled with everything your heart desires: unconditional love, health, beauty, and of course the meeting of all your physical needs. The abundance you envision is indeed yours, it is your Light.

You may say, "As soon as I have settled my affairs, and my finances are in order, and my love life is satisfactory, and I am getting along with my family, I may have the time to open to my Light and learn about such things."

We will reply to you, you have put your cart before your horse [chuckle]. If you were to say to your Light, "I surrender. I will open to you and trust that you will guide me to an awareness of the abundance that you say exists *now* in my universe -- even though I cannot see and know it yet -- I surrender in this moment and I will let my Light carry me. I will trust that my Light will open an awareness of abundance to me."

If you were to say such we will promise you, beloved children -- although we cannot ordain this because we are not your Higher Selves -- we promise you that if you do choose to open your hearts to your Light and know your true nature as beings of Light, you will begin to understand this concept of abundance in all its forms.

: ♦ ♦ :

Human beings will say, "Show me some abundance, prove it to me and then I will trust [chuckle]." And we will say, "Trust and you will know it. Trust it. Trust it and you will know it."

You might say, "Master, my history is replete with lack; lack of love, lack of sustenance, lack of everything that all human beings take as what they need to survive, lack of health. I have not had abundance. How can I know that tomorrow, if I open to my Light and trust it, that it will be otherwise?" You cannot know. You cannot know until you trust it. But it is so. We promise you: This is truth!

We ask you to understand, children, that each of you has co-created your universe. There are no victims here on your plane. There are only human beings who have lived in ignorance, simply because they have not known that they are in a Garden of Eden filled with Light.

You do not know the truth of your reality. You are drowning in your Light. You are drowning in your Light. You do not know that you are loved unconditionally. You do not know that you are cared for in every moment. You do not know that if you simply open your heart and allow, that you can consciously know that you are cared for in every moment. But this is true. This is the reality of your universe. What you have co-created in your suffering is what you believed to be the case. When you are ready to believe something else, you may change what you co-create at any moment.

We understand that what we have spoken may be confusing thoughts for some of you. You might say to us, "Alright, I understand that there is Light and I can partake of it, but in

⋮ ♦ ♦ ⋮

truth, Master, I don't deserve it. I have done terrible things. I have been a terrible person. I have made mistakes."

We would answer, we have not noticed any of that. And the Light simply does not care. This Light only knows how to be beneficent and loving. If you do not feel it, it is because you stop it from being in you. It does not turn away from you. You turn away from it. It only knows how to love you. In truth, this is so.

So you may choose to feel guilt. You may choose to worry and be fearful. After all, you have lived thousands of lifetimes. In many, if not all, of those lifetimes you have known pain. You have known pain in this lifetime. Why should you trust this Light now? Because you are loved!

As time goes by upon your Earth plane and the frequencies increase and shift, you will find that you will have no choice but to trust your Light to carry you through the days and nights. As you allow this to be so you will notice most clearly that you have lost all reason to fear anything. Do you understand?

St. Germain is inviting questions from the audience.

First person: "Is there a difference between feeling dependant on and surrendering to your Light? -- I believe I must give something back to the Light in order to accept anything from it."

St. Germain: What is it that you wish to give back to the Light, child?

: ♦ ♦ :

First person: "I feel at times almost superstitious about the Light, as if I must do things in a special way before I can receive it."

St. Germain: Understand child, being dependant may denote a form of surrender to your Light. It is not the angels and beings of Light upon which you will depend. They are here to assist you, however, as your servants to help you surrender to your own Higher Self, which is your Light.

You are still seeking to set criteria that you must meet as a condition for you to connect to your Light. None are necessary. All that is asked of you is that you open yourself and allow your Light to carry you. This means to be completely dependant upon your Light for guidance and for consciousness while you are in human form. That is where you are all going. You are going to surrender to your Light and understand that the consciousness of your Light is omniscient. It is all-knowing in nature. As you allow this omniscience to guide you, you will then understand how you are cared for in every way by this Light.

Understand, beloved children, you do not need to surrender today, tomorrow, or the next day. You have heard our words and now you may think you must do something. We basically speak of what is happening. This change is already beginning to occur within all of you even as we speak.

We ask you to understand that it is a process. Be kind to yourselves as you move through the process. There is nothing you must do or should do. Just open yourselves to an awareness that this process is occurring. In the moments that are comfortable for you, you may stop and listen and think and

: ◆ ◆ :

know that you are allowing a conscious awareness of the flow of your Light to guide you. You will know that you are allowing the flow because you are feeling comfortable and that this is what it feels like when you are allowing the Light to guide you.

Conversely, when you come to a moment that is uncomfortable, when you are finding that you are still experiencing suffering, worry, anger, or fear you may know then that you have not allowed conscious awareness of your Light. In those times, perhaps you may wish to sit and be still, and with great compassion for yourself love yourself through that moment of discomfort, and know that you can move back to a moment of comfort with your Light when you are ready.

Very often, however, human beings choose self recrimination when they become uncomfortable. They wish to punish themselves, blame themselves, or feel they must ask for forgiveness. All that is really required in those moments, children, is to simply acknowledge that you are uncomfortable. With great compassion, open your heart to feel the discomfort, however it may be. Then ask for help and healing until you may open again to accept this beneficent Light as a conscious awareness. Do you understand?

Please be kind to yourselves in regard to any confusion you may be experiencing. This is not the universe you have been living in. This is the universe you are living in *now*. We ask you to be kind to yourself as you open to these concepts and allow yourself to move into greater awareness and empowerment with the Light. We ask you to consciously know how you are loved. *Know how you are loved.* Perhaps in time you may learn this love for yourself.

: ♦ ♦ :

Second person: What is the true meaning of marriage?

St. Germain: We would like to know this as well [chuckle]. This is not a concept that we have easily adhered to. This concept is predicated upon societal standards. It is an overlay created by human beings -- much the same as war.

This is a societal overlay placed here for two reasons. The woman did not wish the man to roam while she was caring for the children. The man did not wish another man to be the biological father of his children. He wanted to know for sure that they came from his seed. So an agreement was made that they bond, so the man would be certain he was the father and the woman would know that the man would stay to help her care for the children.

Out of this, and of course with the leanings of the human heart, came the desire for permanent mating on your human plane. The ideal became "until death do us part" -- or as we have noted at times, until one kills the other [chuckle].

Understand, beloved children, you are living on a plane of freewill choice. This was part of the choices that came out of chaos when human beings first discovered that they could become yang and yin (male and female) and procreate. What you call your second chakra region [the pelvic area] became a bit of a sticky wicket.

Subsequently, many difficulties ensued. Out of those difficulties came the laws that govern relationships. These laws are superimposed now in a rather uncomfortable setting -- for you see, the balance of yin and yang is changing on your human

: ♦ ♦ :

plane. For a great deal of your history as *homo sapiens* you have existed in a patriarchy. Previous to that it had been a matriarchy. In the days of the matriarchy marriage was not quite as formidable as during the time of the patriarchy.

Now you are moving into a balance of yin and yang and your societal rules regarding marriage have begun to change dramatically as well. A loosening of the ties that bind is occurring on your human plane. What you are noticing at this time is what we have come to recognize as "serial marriage."

As you evolve and heal you may choose more than one partner. At this time in your evolution you are choosing to clear much karma from your previous embodiments, and very quickly so. Thus, the partner you may have chosen in your youth may no longer have karma with you. You may have completed that karma. Now it may be time to move on to your next encounter where more growth may occur.

Of course, this goes against your sensibilities, especially in your western culture, for you were told that you were to marry for life. Thus, you consider the reformation of relationships as a series of failures rather than simply the evolution of your being to greater Light.

Understand, children, when you choose the act of sex you are profoundly mixing your chakra energy with the energy of another human. If your frequencies are changing, as you are opening to your Light, and your partner is not choosing similar growth, the dissonance and disharmony between you will only increase dramatically. In this age of rapid growth, this will become even more uncomfortable.

: ♦ ♦ :

To stay in a similar frequency with another human is a very difficult and challenging thing to do since no two beings will have the same path of growth and awakening. You are all very unique beings of Light and so your paths will be unique as well. Thus, simultaneous growth with another human will be quite a challenge.

We ask you to be kind to yourselves if you have found that your frequencies are no longer harmonic. Acknowledge that perhaps it is time to move into a celibate state until the fundamental laws that govern "like attracting like" will bring you to another being who has a similar frequency to you. Perhaps then you may join again in partnership to move to even greater growth.

The institution that you call marriage -- along with all the institutions on your human plane -- are moving to new paradigms now. You have noticed your government, your education, your health care, all institutions are reforming. They *must* as the energies shift on your Earth plane. And this is true for marriage as well.

We are grateful that we have been of service to you all. Allow your hearts to be open, children, and know that you are loved.

: ♦ ♦ :　　: ♦ ♦ :　　: ♦ ♦ :

: ♦ ♦ :

Ascended Masters Newsletter # 9

Aggression, Anger, Fear, and Speaking Your Truth

This message comes from El Morya Khan, the Ascended Master associated with the Blue Ray. In preparation we were asked to allow a stream of luminous blue Light to enter the wheel of Light at our throat chakra. The blue Light can help us heal the throat chakra that often holds issues of judgment of self or others. The blue Light can also aid us in speaking our truth or healing a sense of overwhelm.

Beloved children, this is a time, more so than ever before, when you as human beings may choose to be consciously aware of your personal truth that resonates within you. Indeed, each one of you may find that your truth may vary from the truths of others around you. Of course, your first thought in response to this may be, "What is he or she thinking? How can they possibly be correct?" From *your* perspective at the center of *your* universe only one opinion can be correct -- and that would be *yours*.

Although you may not judge harshly the choices of others and the truths that they may choose to speak, you may hold a perspective that is at odds with theirs. A combative stance may ensue when you realize that who you are and what you believe is at odds with others around you. Anger may arise within you because others do not agree with or understand your truth. Simultaneously, you may feel a greater need to speak up. A

: ♦ ♦ :

combative stance and a desire to fight back may develop within you.

However, you are finding at this time that being angry and fighting back when others do not agree with your perspective, your ideas, or your view of the world may not have the desired results anymore. More and more, the tactics you have used in the past to express your disagreement are, in effect, backfiring. There does not appear to be the satisfaction that you once enjoyed from these behaviors. By backfiring we mean that speaking what you deem to be your truth, if it comes from a source of anger, may make you feel worse instead of better.

In the days to come, a direct approach that involves anger may not at all be an effective way to speak your truth on this planet. Anger as you have known it, aggression as you have known it, fighting as you have known it, and, indeed, war as you have known it are energies that are losing their power to be effective in changing your world in a direction of your liking.

For those of you who understand the astrological configurations currently occurring in your heavens, everything we speak of here is related to these particular configurations [El Morya Khan is referring to retrograde Mars in Pisces]. In the heavens you can indeed see the pattern of what is occurring on Earth. "As above, so below."

When you use anger in response now, the results will invariably be disappointing. While these have never been "positive" energies for change, in the past they have, at least from time to time, effectively created change that might appear satisfactory to you. *Now and in the days to come the energies of aggression, anger, war, or fighting of any sort will not lead to anything at*

: ♦ ♦ :

all approaching a positive resolution in any given situation. We do not ordain this, we simply explain the situation as it exists.

Why do we speak of these things? Your planet is moving very rapidly into frequencies which Leia and Manalus have chosen to describe as the fourth dimension. Indeed, a new dimensional energy is available to you -- and other dimensional energies will follow quickly on the heels of this energy. You and your planet are moving very rapidly into opportunities to create new ways of being that will be far more harmonious to you than that of which we have just spoken.

You may say to us, "Master, I still feel anger. I still become angry and wish to speak angry words. And I wish to wage my own wars from time to time. What could you suggest that would be a more useful pattern for these energies?" You may even say, "I still enjoy feeling angry from time to time and I feel it is important to express my angry feelings. I do not wish to let go of my anger or the perspective that has led to my anger."

Beloved children, we are not here to tell you that you *must* do *anything*. We have come as harbingers of the new era that is developing upon your human plane and to speak of it to you. What you choose to do in response, we honor completely. We can only love you unconditionally and support you in any choices you may make in the days to come. If you do not find this information useful, so be it. We honor and love you still. If you *do* find this information useful then we are most grateful to be of service to you at this time.

Let us tell you what might prove a useful alternative to the third-dimensional energies that you have not only carried in this lifetime, but many lifetimes prior to this incarnation. What you

⋮ ♦ ♦ ⋮

may wish to understand is that being angry, in and of itself, is not a terrible thing. We do not encourage you to stop being angry. We know that being on the human plane on any given day can be a very frustrating experience. We hear this very often from the human beings with whom we are connected. First and foremost, have compassion for yourselves for what you are experiencing.

We have been telling you, "Nothing is as it has been nor as it will be." This means, beloved children, that everything you have known in this and in all other of your lifetimes no longer applies. All historic precedence is falling away. In time, you will find that every paradigm in which you have functioned to this time is no longer applicable to the universe in which you will choose to reside. This can be frustrating indeed if all the tools that you have used to navigate your universe are no longer as useful as they once were. This can be very exhausting and, at times, very frightening. Frustration is a form of anger and, of course, anger comes from fear.

We encourage you to acknowledge your anger when you feel the discomfort of it. But we ask you to do this *as you sit and are still*. Then acknowledge the emotion and feelings that are coming to your awareness. We ask you to consider doing this *without judging yourselves*.

At this point you may say, "Master, it was not my intention to judge myself, it was my intention to judge the situation or human that has produced this anger within me." We would respond, *no one and nothing can make you angry*. You may *choose* to become angry in response to a stimulus in your environment, but please remember, beloved children, that no one and nothing can make you angry.

: ◆ ◆ :

If anything will raise anger within you, it is the *fear* a situation is triggering within you -- based on previous experiences in this lifetime or in another lifetime -- that is being reactivated by that situation. You have become frightened. That is the only reason that you will become angry. Therefore we ask you to have compassion for yourself regarding whatever fear has come to you. You may not actually have an understanding of the fear, but know that it is there. Then ask the Light to help you heal your fears and, most importantly, trust that the Light can help with your fears more so than ever before.

Be aware that the times in which you have chosen to live are specifically designed by all of you who have chosen to be alive to bring to the surface all the fears that you have not wished to acknowledge to this time. If you have unresolved fears, anger, or emotional pain within your being, this is the time to look at your deepest feelings and bring them to the surface. This is likely to create anger within you, for you do not wish to be afraid. But it will also offer you the opportunity to heal these feelings.

As you heal with the Light and allow the Light to do this work, you will find that *compassion for yourself* arises within your heart. Furthermore, you will find that your heart is now open to feeling *compassion for the world around you*. This can bring you to a new place that very quickly gains you entry into the energies of the fourth dimension. As you grow into compassion and its companion asset -- wisdom -- you will find that growing within you is an unconditional love for yourself.

At first you may decry what is occurring on your human plane at this time. But we ask you to be aware that what is occurring

: ♦ ♦ :

is a situation that is offering you, if you allow it, the Light of Infinite Source to bring healing into your life.

We counsel you that when you are feeling pain and discomfort, realize that what has brought up these feelings and emotions within you is the very Light that is loving and nurturing you. Then speak within your hearts, *"This is the Light of Source healing me now."* We would encourage you to affirm this phrase as you feel the pain: *"This is the Light of Source healing me now."* You may find this to be a far more useful method of dealing with the discomfort in your environment than resorting to aggression.

This does not mean, beloved children, that we do not encourage you to speak your truth. *All we ask of you is that you sit and be still to know it first!* You may be surprised at the truth that you find within. You may indeed be surprised.

And so we offer you all the greatest love and Light and wish you well on your journey.

: ♦ ♦ :   : ♦ ♦ :   : ♦ ♦ :

: ♦ ♦ :

Ascended Masters Newsletter # 10

Realize Your Sovereignty as Co-Creators of Your Universe

We welcome you, beloved children, to this opportunity for conscious communication. Please know, however, that this is not the only time that we communicate with you. In your time alone, when you sit with your Light, we are with you then as well as now.

You may not fully accept that you are communicating with the Light. You may believe that some human beings can do this more easily than others. That is not true at all. Each and every being who dwells upon your plane -- the lowliest ant or insect that you believe is a lesser form of intelligence than you are, the eagle soaring through your sky, the leopard walking in its jungle, the mountain lion roaring its sovereignty in its domain, the trees that whisper in the breeze, the air that blows past you, the Earth upon which you walk -- all are connected and filled with this Light. All are channeling this Light through every particle of their beings. Even an object that appears inert such as a stone is, of course, radiating Light. You can see this easily in what you consider the higher forms of crystals. You can feel energy flowing through those crystals. That is the Light of Source flowing through everything.

You are aware that the atomic structure that informs everything on the gross material plane is in constant motion. But let us take you beyond the atomic level. As you know, the atom is a

: ♦ :

composition of many parts. If you strip away the various parts of the atom, and reduce these parts even further, there is more that exists there, more life that is made animate by the Light. Your scientists know that these smaller particles, as they call them, do not move unless they are observed.

Consciousness informs your planet. The Light flows through it. When consciousness occurs, a connection is made. Energy channels through all life that you observe *when* you observe it. Light is in everything. Light is the life force of the universe -- and yet *there is no movement in your universe unless it is observed.* An interesting thought, is it not?

What we are asking you to understand is that you are sovereign in your universe. You sit in the center of the universe that you observe and *as you observe it, it exists.* It becomes alive. It becomes animated. *You* create this animation in your universe. Granted, it all exists. It all carries the life force of the Light. And yet, you co-create what you observe. Your focus brings your universe to life. That is a powerful piece of information.

All of you have been created as beings of Light walking in human form on this planet. And if you understand the power of the Light you carry, then you can know that you co-create the planet upon which you choose to exist.

What do you want in your universe, children? Do you want strife, suffering, worry, fear, difficulties? Do you want malnourishment? Do you want physical infirmity? Do you want aging? Do you want death? Do you want war? Do you want peace? Do you want gentle, kindly behavior or difficult and angry experiences?

: ◆ ◆ :

However, you may say to us, "Master, we truly believe we have no control over what we observe in our universe. Things happen that really seem beyond our control." We would ask you, what is it that you wish to control? Do you wish to be in a state of well being? Or do you wish to suffer? What do you want in your universe? What do you want to observe? What to you want to experience? You decide. You choose.

This may appear very heady information indeed -- and we would agree with you. What we are telling you may seem to be more than you wish to know with your human mind. For it is much easier for human beings to blame others for their discomfort than to own it for themselves. It is much easier for them to say, "Well, where I live there is drought and no food. People are starving." Or, "Where I live there is war. My family has been murdered. How did I choose such an experience?"

We would answer that the reasons these things have happened are far more complex than you can know with your human mind. You cannot know all the reasons why you choose an experience. But one thing is certain. If you are having such an experience we ask you to have compassion for yourself because you simply do not know yet that you are sovereign in your universe. Once you understand your sovereignty, and that you co-create your universe, you may wish to know how you can change the circumstances of your life.

Now more than ever this knowledge is available to human beings. It has never been known before as it can be known now. More so than ever before it is now possible to co-create consciously what you choose to experience here on your land, in your world, on Mother Earth.

: ◆ ◆ :

The veils are thinning between the planes. The higher-vibrational frequencies are more easily available to you. You can now know things that you never dreamt would be accessible with your conscious human mind. You can co-create your universe to be in balance and harmony. You can co-create that your body is healthy, that your life is productive, and that you are free of suffering.

You may say, "If this is so then why is it that I observe other human beings around me still choosing to suffer? Even if I am well, I can still see in my universe that others are not choosing the same degree of wellness. Knowing this causes pain in my heart." We would answer, so be it. Indeed, you may choose to suffer with others. But does that help them heal? Would it not be more useful to heal the pain in your heart, return to balance and harmony, and share your loving radiance of Light with those who are suffering in the world around you?

If you say that you cannot be happy until everyone else is happy then everyone will have a long wait for happiness. Happiness does not come from waiting for others to be happy. Nor does it come from material gain, or adulation of others, or physical beauty, or acquisition of things. All that your society tells you will make you happy -- find the right fellow, find the right lady, and so forth and so on -- these things will not make you happy.

There is only one place where you will most certainly find happiness: When you sit with your Light, open your heart, and allow this unconditionally loving Light to fill your being and radiate throughout you. Then share this Light with others. That will bring you happiness. Sit in your Light, allow it to saturate your being with this loving energy, and radiate it to all who come to you. That will transform your universe and bring you

: ♦ ♦ :

peace, balance and harmony. In so doing you will be channeling the Light.

Each and every one of you can do this. It is very much an equal opportunity experience. There is only one thing that can stop you from staying in balance and harmony, and from living in a universe that is balanced and harmonious, and that is if you believe that this cannot be so for you. If prior to this time you have had much suffering in your life and you believe that is your lot then that is what you will have.

You may say that there has been suffering in your life -- and every human being can say this -- and that there is suffering on the human plane. However, if you know within your heart that you are a being of Light in human form; if you know that every place you rest your eyes, there also exists the Light; if you can recognize the Light in every piece of rock, in every creature that walks upon your Earth, in a blade of grass, in the wind that blows past you, in the trees, in the Earth; if you lift the veil from your eyes and know the truth, which is *all is Light*; if you choose to recognize this Light in everything you see, even the great leaders of your country, if you can see them as Light, then indeed you have found your sovereignty in your universe and all is in balance and in harmony. *All is Light*.

You may ask, "Master, why am I here upon this Earth? Why did I want to be alive at this time?" *The reason why you have chosen to be alive at this time is to be your Light, to radiate your Light and to see your Light in everyone and everything.*

We ask you to do this without expectation. Realize, however, that if you infuse an awareness and focus of Light in everything as you observe it, it transforms your experience of it. Even if

: ♦ ♦ :

what you are observing in this fashion is at a distance, you have consciously contributed to the transformation of that portion of your universe. That is the power that you possess now. Do you understand?

Conversely, because you carry great power, if you decide that you are observing something in your universe that is not of Light, that is terrible, unfortunate, bad, wrong, judging it in whatever way you choose to judge it, that experience will be devoid of this harmonic energy. You will not be sending Light, and whatever thoughts you do have that are disharmonious will be the energy that you send to that experience.

We ask you, beloved children, sit in the center of your universe, observe yourself as a being of Light. Feel the Light filling your form. Let it enter through the wheel of Light at your heart that is the seat of your wisdom. (Wisdom is not in your mind; it is in your heart.) Feel the unconditionally loving Light of Source filling your heart. Let it radiate throughout your form, nurturing and loving you in this moment. And then think of a situation that you find harmonious and joyful and send love and feelings of radiance and expansion toward it. Does that not enhance your being and strengthen your Light? Whatever you observe and send Light to will reflect back to you. It will fill you with even more Light.

Now we ask you to lift your focus and think of a situation that is perhaps less harmonic, a time when you had some uncomfortable thoughts. What happens to the Light that is filling your form? Does it not lessen within you when you have these thoughts? Now choose to recognize the Light in that situation, whatever it is. Choose to once again fill your heart consciously with the Light of Source and recognize and

: ♦ ♦ :

commune with the Light that is in the "uncomfortable" situation. *Know* that the Light is in *every* situation. Allow yourself the conscious experience of connecting with that Light. Strengthen it and aid the radiation of Light within whatever it is that you are focusing upon. Does this not strengthen the Light within you?

Understand children, when you choose to see everything in your universe as Light, that nourishes you. Conversely, when you choose to evaluate or judge a situation as less than this glorious radiance of Light, it does not nourish you; instead, it diminishes the Light within you. -- Seeing all as Light is a selfish act, is it not?

Please understand the sovereignty that you carry as beings of Light in co-creating your universe. Understand that it is useless to blame others for your unhappiness. No matter what another chooses to do, rather than feeling uncomfortable with his or her choice, you may choose to recognize that they, too, are beings of Light. See them as such and keep your heart open to radiate Light in response -- anything else will diminish you.

This Light is your most precious attribute. More precious than all the wealth of your human plane. It is truly your abundance.

We understand there may be questions. Of course, we are here to be of service.

Question: *Do you want to encourage others to channel for themselves?*

Answer: It is simply what shall happen for each and every being upon this plane. All will be in direct communication with the

: ♦ ♦ :

Light. Even if they are not yet allowing conscious communication, they are, in fact, in direct communication with their Totalities (or Higher Selves). That is what informs each being and animates it. But if a human being chooses to stay embodied in the days to come this conscious communication will spontaneously occur for each and every one. It must be so.

Question: *How long do we have to stay in a body for that to happen?*

Answer: It is happening now for the one who has asked [a lady of 85 years]. It may be difficult for you to accept the reality of it, but in each and every moment you are communicating with your Totality and radiating this Light to your plane. Even if it is a simple task such as going into your garden and touching the fruits of your labor, that is a direct communication from your Totality to enjoy the bounty of this plane and the fruits of it. You may be looking for something more profound, but truly it is the simple things that bring joy. You have learned how to create a life that is joyful and that is a direct communication with your Totality. Is it not wondrous indeed? All those who know you, know you do this, but it is still difficult for you to believe for yourself. As you pet your creatures and feel your love touch their hearts, and their love touch yours, you can know that this is your Light directly expressing itself through you. You give your gifts of love freely. That is your Light expressing itself through you, daughter, in every moment.[5]

:♦ ♦:   :♦ ♦:   :♦ ♦:

---

[5] If you wish to subscribe to the Ascended Masters Newsletter, please send an e-mail to that effect to expansion@u-r-light.com.

:♦ ♦:

Books by the Authors

Expansion Publishing is offering the following titles by Linda Stein-Luthke and Martin F. Luthke, Ph.D.:

• *Angels and Other Beings of Light: They are Here to Help You! A Discourse from the Ascended Master St. Germain,* by Linda Stein-Luthke and Martin F. Luthke, ISBN 0-9656927-3-6, 84 pp., US $8.95. A channeled discourse on working with angels, Archangels, Ascended Masters, Twin Flame, soul mates, and other beings of Light; who they are; what their purpose is; how to contact them; how to experience your Higher Self; suggested readings.

• *Balancing the Light Within. A Discourse on Healing from the Ascended Master St. Germain,* by Linda Stein-Luthke and Martin F. Luthke, ISBN 0-9656927-0-1, 54 pp., US $6.95. A channeled discourse on light vibrations, tools of awareness, chakras, healing of self and others with metaphysical means; suggested readings.

• *Affirmations and Thought Forms: You Can Change Your Mind! A Discourse from the Ascended Master St. Germain,* by Linda Stein-Luthke and Martin F. Luthke, ISBN 0-9656927-1-X, 48 pp., US $6.95. A channeled discourse on the use of affirmations and the power of thought forms and how to use both for healing purposes, with emphasis on self-empowerment and self-awareness; suggested readings.

⋮ ◆ ◆ ⋮

- **_Riding the Tide of Change: Preparing for Personal &_**
Planetary Transformation, by Martin F. Luthke, ISBN 0-9656927-2-8, 108 pp., US $9.95. A metaphysical book on Earth changes with an emphasis on releasing fears, healing self and understanding our role as co-creators during this time of transformation; suggested readings.

- **_Beyond Psychotherapy: Introduction to Psychoenergetic_**
Healing, by Martin F. Luthke and Linda Stein-Luthke, ISBN 0-9656927-4-4, 228 pp., US $19.95. This book by the founders of Psychoenergetic Healing describes an advanced approach to the healing of emotional, mental, spiritual and physical issues. A groundbreaking introduction for healers, psychotherapists and all who are interested in energy-based healing methods.

- **_Navigating the Fourth Dimension:_** _A Discourse from the Ascended Masters St. Germain and El Morya Khan,_ by Linda Stein-Luthke and Martin F. Luthke, ISBN 0-9656927-5-2, 134 pp., US $11.95. A channeled discourse explaining why the past no longer applies and proposing new ways of thinking, being and creating that can lead to an experience of harmony, balance, peace and abundance in the here and now. The appendix contains the first ten issues of the Ascended Masters Newsletter.

⋮◆◆⋮   ⋮◆◆⋮   ⋮◆◆⋮

⋮◆◆⋮

How to Order Books

- **For more information**: For more information, excerpts, and secure on-line orders, please visit *www.u-r-light.com*. You may e-mail any inquiries to *expansion@u-r-light.com*. Please contact us for overseas orders or quantity discounts.

- **On-line orders**: Please visit http://*www.u-r-light.com*.

- **Mail-in orders**: Please send your order -- including your e-mail address, if available -- to: Expansion Publishing, P.O. Box 516, Chagrin Falls, OH 44022, USA. Shipping: Please add $2.00 for orders totaling up to $10 and $4.00 for orders over $10. US-checks or money orders.

- **Bookstores**: All titles are also available through your local bookstore. However, you may need to special-order them.

- **Phone orders**: Please call **Book Clearing House** (800-356-9315) for 24-hour credit card orders.

:♦ ♦:   :♦ ♦:   :♦ ♦:

:♦ ♦: